BASKETBALL FOR WOMEN

Physical Education Activities Series

Frances Schaafsma
California State University at Long Beach

Photography by Nancy Kepley

THIRD EDITION

Wm C Brown Company Publishers
Dubuque, Iowa

Consulting Editor

Aileene Lockhart
Texas Woman's University

Evaluation Materials Editor

Jane A. Mott
Texas Woman's University

Copyright © 1966, 1971, 1977 by Wm. C. Brown Company Publishers

Library of Congress Catalog Card Number: 76-27779

ISBN 0—697—07074-3

Printed in the United States of America

BASKETBALL
FOR WOMEN

About the author

Dr. Frances Schaafsma is a Professor of Physical Education and Associate Director for Sports, Athletics, and Recreation at California State University at Long Beach. She earned her bachelor's and master's degrees at California State University at Long Beach and her Ph.D. at the University of Southern California. Dr. Schaafsma has coached women's basketball at California State University at Long Beach from 1962 to the present. During that time her teams have had a record of 154 wins and 46 losses and have participated in AIAW National Basketball Championships in 1972, 1973, and 1976. In addition, she coached varsity volleyball, also at CSULB, from 1962-1971.

Dr. Schaafsma has been active in women's sports as a player, official, and coach throughout her career. She has served in numerous elected and appointed positions in women's sports organizations, including the first Commissioner for National Championships of the Commission for Intercollegiate Athletics for Women from 1968-1970. She is currently President-elect for the Western Association for Intercollegiate Athletics for Women. She has also found time to conduct coaching clinics in basketball throughout the United States.

Besides authoring three editions of *Basketball for Women* for WCB, Dr. Schaafsma has also coauthored two other books published by WCB: *Volleyball* and *Volleyball for Coaches and Teachers*.

Contents

Preface vii

1. What Basketball Is Like 1

2. What Every Player Should Know 8

3. Skills Essential for Everyone 15

4. Better Players Master These Techniques 33

5. Basic Concepts for Offensive and Defensive Action ... 40

6. Patterns of Offensive Play 42

7. Patterns of Defensive Play 61

8. Game Situations 68

9. Rules of the Game 72

    Appendix: Questions and Answers 79

    Index 86

Preface

This book is designed for the beginning and intermediate student of the game of basketball. Though written toward the student, it also should be of value to the teacher of beginning classes and the coach of junior high and high school teams.

It is designed to provide a study of the basic skills, techniques, and strategies of basketball. The fundamentals necessary for building offensive and defensive play are also covered specifically. Though the brevity of the text precludes the possibility of investigating complex aspects of advanced play in detail, it is hoped that this book will aid the reader in bridging the gap between merely playing and playing with real understanding.

As one who has experienced, from the point of view of both player and coach, the evolution of women's basketball from three-court through two-court and roving player to its current form, much analysis and learning about the game has occurred on my part. I am especially grateful for all those teammates, players, and students who have questioned and analyzed with me through the years in order to gain more understanding.

Acknowledgement is also made to Debbie Cantu, Monica Havelka, Barbara Mosher, Karen Noel, Linda Russell, Lynne Stith, and Cathy Sutton, players at California State University, Long Beach from 1975 through 1977, who served as models for the photographs illustrating skills and strategies.

Frances Schaafsma

What basketball is like

1

The game of basketball is fast and exciting, for it involves almost continuous movement and action. These ingredients make it challenging in many ways for the participant and a thrilling experience for the spectator.

The prime objective of the game is to score more points than one's opponent by pushing, throwing, or tossing a leather- or rubber-covered ball with a 9 1/2-inch diameter through the goal. This goal has an 18-inch diameter ring, which is attached to a backboard and placed 10 feet above the level of the court.

The game is contested between 2 teams, each comprised of 5 players. Each team has its own goal at opposite ends of a court area, which measures approximately 94 feet by 50 feet.

To begin the game an official tosses the ball upward between two opponents at the center of the court area. From this toss, both players attempt to tap the ball to one of their respective teammates. After one team gains possession of the ball, the game proceeds as teammates move the ball toward their own goal and attempt to score, while their opponents try to defend against this effort. During the entire game neither team is permitted to make significant physical contact with members of the opposing team. The ball may be moved about the court by passing, throwing, or bouncing it to teammates, or it may be bounced to oneself in a sequence of bounces.

HISTORY

The first game of basketball was played at Springfield College in Springfield, Massachusetts, in 1891, as the invention of Dr. James Naismith. The goal was a peach basket and the first ball a soccer ball. The game grew rapidly in popularity after it was demonstrated by two teams (captained by Amos

Alonzo Stagg and Naismith himself) at a YMCA conference in 1892. Women, too, played the game almost immediately, the first known college game being at Smith College that same year. The first women's rule book was published in 1899.
in popularity after it was demonstrated by two teams (captained by Amos
The evolution of today's rules is an interesting story. Early basketball was a good deal slower and less strenuous than today's game. From a court divided into three playing zones, the game progressed to the half-court game still remembered by many. The objective of the game as a noncontact sport has not changed appreciably, but the speed of the game has been altered drastically. Originally only one bounce was permitted; this progressed to two, then later to three. In addition, the adoption of the roving player game under a standard set of rules for both the Division for Girls and Women's Sports and the Amateur Athletic Union in 1962 was a giant stride toward making basketball a more exciting game for women. The adoption of the full-court, five-player game occurred in 1971, bringing women's basketball to the stage it is in today.

CURRENT TRENDS

Interscholastic and intercollegiate basketball has grown throughout the United States in recent years, with league and tournament play occurring at both the local and regional levels. The Division for Girls and Women's Sports conducted the first National Intercollegiate Basketball Championships at Illinois State University in the Spring of 1972. With the organization of the Association of Intercollegiate Athletics for Women, the National Intercollegiate Basketball Championships are now played under the auspices of this organization. Teams qualify by winning state championships and then placing first or second in the Regional Championships held in the nine regions of AIAW.

Basketball is played by women throughout the world. Teams play throughout Canada, Central America, South America, and the European and Middle East countries. Rules governing play vary in degrees from country to country. Women's basketball has been played in the Pan-American Games for years and were played in the 1976 Olympic Games in Montreal, Canada for the first time. International play has been frequent in recent years as all-star teams from various countries have made playing tours and as World Games competition has come into being. The Russian women's teams have dominated most of the international play to date. A recent addition to competition for women has been the inception of the World University Games. In the summer of 1973 an outstanding team of USA college and university women placed second to Russia in the Games held in Moscow. The 1975 Games were cancelled due to the inability of the host country, Bulgaria, to finalize the arrangements for the competition. The World University Games are normally conducted the year following and the year prior to the Olympic Games.

In international play the rules used are those used in the Olympic Games. These rules differ a great deal from those most commonly used in the United

---

Do you know when women first played basketball in the Olympic Games? What other international competition in basketball is open to women?

States. Much more physical contact is permitted than is customary in either women's or men's play in the United States. In addition free throws are only taken for fouls made against a player in the act of shooting.

Basketball rules seem to change quite often. This is primarily a result of the changes that occur in playing techniques and strategies. Changes in wording or additional rules are sometimes necessary to insure player safety or to maintain a situation conducive to fair play. Other changes in girls' and women's basketball have occurred as a result of changes in the concepts of the physical capabilities of women.

The National Association for Girls and Women's Sports (formerly the Division for Girls and Women's Sports) and the Women's Basketball Committee of the Amateur Athletic Union jointly make a yearly study of the rules. Any interested person may make suggestions for rules changes to the rules committee chairman listed in the current guide. Alterations in the rules are made only after careful study of the need for the change, as well as the effect of such a change. Much experimentation takes place and the reactions of players, teachers, coaches, and officials are carefully considered before any change is put into effect.

PREPARING TO PLAY

Basketball is easily one of the most inexpensive sports in which to participate. The only *equipment* necessary is a ball and a court. The *ball* should be selected in accordance with the type of use it will be given. Out-of-doors play requires a rubber- or composition-covered ball. Indoor play can be conducted with either leather or rubber; the leather ball, however, will be damaged very quickly in outdoor play.

The *court* should have a good traction surface and should be clearly marked. This may require special mopping care for indoor courts. Outdoor courts should be swept frequently to eliminate an accumulation of dust. All courts should have a 4- to 6-foot clearance from the boundaries, especially directly under the baskets.

Your *costume* for play should allow freedom of movement. If your team is to play a game, all players should be in identical and appropriate dress, with large identifying numbers on both the front and the back of the blouse.

Take special care to see that your *rubber-soled shoes* are laced properly. If the shoes have been worn on dust, dirt, or grass surfaces, it will be necessary to clean them carefully to remove all residue that could cause slipping on the court.

Can you identify these terms frequently heard on the basketball court: free-lance, gunner, hot-hand, give and go, cripple, and solo?

WHERE TO PLAY

Many opportunities are available for those who would like to play basketball, whether on the beginning, intermediate, or advanced level. One of the distinct advantages of this game over other team sports is that it can be played alone. You can purchase a rubber basketball for approximately $10.00, a goal for a similar amount, and construct a backboard with discarded lumber. A good pair of basketball shoes can be purchased for $5.00 to $8.00 and you are ready to play. Quite a number of shooting games are available to the individual who wants to shoot alone in the backyard. Most playgrounds throughout the country have basketball goals and most schools and colleges have gymnasiums that are open daily, thus providing many opportunities for shooting and playing the game.

For the beginner, most opportunities for playing will come on the playground with other novices. It is rather easy to find three or four other players who would like to play two-on-two or three-on-three. Enough players will often be available for five-on-five. When three-on-three is played, usually only one goal is used while five-on-five is usually played on full court.

As you improve your play, you may find that you will have the opportunity to play on your school team, either varsity or junior varsity. If you have a desire to play, most coaches will be eager to have you come out for their team, and if you are not good enough for their varsity, will be pleased to have you play junior-varsity basketball. If your skill is not advanced enough for play on this level, then be sure to participate in the intramural program at your school.

If you are not in school, you will find many opportunities for play in playground leagues, church leagues, or YMCA leagues. Check with your local recreation department or your local YMCA for full information as to what leagues are available.

Basketball is played year round and facilities for the game are improving constantly. If you have a sincere desire to play the game, you will have no trouble finding opportunities. Work at the game daily and play as often as possible and you will be pleasantly surprised at the results you will accomplish.

LANGUAGE OF THE GAME

Familiarity with the following *terms* will assist you in becoming a knowledgeable player and spectator. Some of the terms are technical in nature and are used to describe various aspects of the game. Others are descriptive colloquialisms in use by players, coaches, sportswriters, and sports announcers.

Assist. To pass to an open teammate, this action resulting in an immediate score.

If you would like to propose a change in the basketball rules, do you know to whom your suggestion should be sent? Which organizations are responsible for studying possible changes and instituting those that seem desirable?

Backcourt. That half of the court in which a team plays defense, or the part of the frontcourt nearer the centerline of the court.

Ball control. A type of play that emphasizes maintaining possession of the ball until a sure shot is possible. The other team cannot score without the ball.

Cripple. An unguarded shot close to the basket that should be scored 100 percent of the time.

Cut-in. A quick movement into an open space, usually to receive the ball for an unguarded shot.

Defense. The team attempting to keep its opponent from scoring.

Double-team. To place two defensive players in position to guard the player with the ball (usually a temporary measure).

Dribble. Successive bounces of the ball, in which each bounce after the first must be executed by one hand only.

Drive. A quick, hard dribbling movement of a player with the ball as she goes toward the basket.

Fake. A decoy or feinting movement designed to draw an opponent out of position.

Fall-away. A method of performing certain shots and passes in which the player with the ball moves one direction as the ball moves another.

Feint. Nothing more than a fake.

Fast break. After taking possession of the ball at the defensive end of the floor, to make a rapid attack on the opponents' goal before they can recover into a defensive position.

Free-lance. A type of offense in which players attempt to take advantage of whatever openings may occur; players utilize basic one-on-one and two-on-two.

Frontcourt. That half of the court in which a team plays offense, or the part of the court closer to a team's goal.

Give and go. A team effort on offense that consists of passing the ball to a teammate (the give) and moving into an opening to take a return pass (the go).

Gunner. A player who likes to shoot and does so almost every time she gets the ball.

Hook shot (pass). Turning the nonshooting side of the body toward the guard, the player shoots or passes over the defender, the ball being released high overhead as the arm makes a circular path.

Hot hand. Possessed by the shooter who makes almost any shot she attempts.

Jump shot (pass). Difficult to guard, this shot (or pass) is released well overhead after its thrower has jumped high into the air.

Lay-up. A shot for goal taken at very close range after a dribble or cut for the basket. The ball is softly placed over the rim or against the backboard so that it will rebound into the basket.

Moves. The combination of fakes and movements that makes a player more successful in evading an opponent's attempt to guard her.

Offense. The team in possession of the ball.

One-on-one. The balance of one defensive player on one offensive player, with neither having a teammate nearby. Similar offense to defense ratios are expressed, such as "two-on-two," "three-on-two," "four-on-four," etc.

Pattern play. Offensive play designed to give a team successive and optional openings for shots. The offensive players move in a prescribed direction and at a preplanned time to draw the defense into positions that may create opportunities for shots. The options are selected on the basis of what the defense does.

Percentage play (shot). An attempt to take the shot that has the best chance of going into the basket. In general, the closer the shooter is to the basket the better her chances of scoring. The chances are more limited if the player is either off balance or well guarded or if the shooting team has no one near the goal to rebound.

Pick-off. Any time a defensive player cannot follow her opponent as she moves because she cannot get through "the crowd" of either opponents or teammates. The pick-off can be either an intentional barrier set by an opponent or the act of the offensive player using an opportune occurrence.

Pivot. A movement in place with one foot remaining stationary or an offensive play pattern that uses one player as a hub for passes and return passes as teammates cut toward the basket.

Player-to-player. A defensive alignment in which each player is assigned to defend against one specific offensive opponent.

Post. When a player acts as the pivot player in the pivot pattern she is said to be playing the "post." A "high post" player positions 12 to 18 feet from the basket. A "low post" positions 8 to 10 feet from the basket.

Press. A defensive attempt to force an opponent into making some kind of error, thus giving up the ball. It is usually accomplished by aggressive defense, double-teaming, or harrassing the ball handler with attempts to tie the ball. The press can be applied full-court, half-court, or any other fractional part of the playing area.

Screen. A human partition set by one offensive player placing herself in front of a teammate's opponent so that the ball handler may have an open shot or opportunity to move.

Set shot. Any shot taken from a stationary position.

Solo. A one-player offensive effort, which may be accompanied by teammates positioning so as not to interfere.

Turnover. To commit an error, make a violation, or make a bad pass, any of which results in a loss of ball possession without having had a chance to shoot for the goal.

Zone. Any type of defense that begins with players assigned to cover specific areas of the court, rather than specific persons. The zone may be bounded by certain imaginary lines or it may be a zone relationship of players who will shift on the court.

What every player should
know

2

Since basketball requires almost constant movement and because players move quickly in limited space, you will need to concentrate on developing good body control. Next you must work to attain muscular and cardiorespiratory endurance.

Then to really enjoy playing the game, you will need to develop proficiency in the skills of ball handling, shooting for goals, and defending against opponents' play.

Like most team games, basketball requires good coordination among teammates while on both offense and defense. Though offensive team patterns can be extremely simple yet effective, they can also be developed to a level approaching that of the intricate choreography of the dance. Defensive team play is a combination of attempting to coordinate as a unit yet individually anticipate the opponents' intentions and movements. In both offensive and defensive play, quick thinking and the ability to make split-second adjustments and compensations are vital. Mastery of these as a team requires practice, but will be rewarded with much satisfaction. Team play in basketball resembles the intrigue of a chess game, with the offense attempting to lure the defense into a given position from which the offense can then gain an advantage and score. On the other hand, the defense is constantly on the alert to detect the decoy movements and counteract with plays to foil the attack.

Basketball is an American-originated game that has interested a great many boys and girls and men and women throughout this country for many years. Its popularity is increasing and expanding constantly, so that the game is now played throughout the world. It is played as an interschool, intercollegiate, and professional sport; it is played by youngsters of all ages in schools and on playgrounds, by all ages and types of groups in recreational programs, and by a vast number of girls and women throughout the country who enjoy vigorous, skillful activity.

You will find that when you have mastered the fundamental skills of the game, you will gain a feeling of well-being, not only as a result of the fine physical conditioning you will develop but through experiencing the team play, through the challenge of out-thinking opponents, and through developing the self-control and fair play that are integral parts of this fun game—basketball.

The next sections of this chapter outline some of physical, mental, and emotional prerequisites for improving play. Discussions of individual skills and team tactics are covered in succeeding chapters.

MENTAL PREPARATION FOR PLAY

There is no shortcut to the mastery of the various skills and strategies of basketball, but much advantage can be gained by appropriate mental preparation for learning, practice, and competition.

Concentration

Concentration is a primary factor necessary for success in any sport requiring skill. For the individual to be able to concentrate to the maximum, skills must be developed to a stage of automatic response, so that the mental focus is on *what* to do and not *how* to do it. To reach this stage, learning and repetition of the skill or strategy are required in as gamelike a situation as possible. There is no substitute for practice in bringing an individual to the state of mental freedom that allows all energies to be focused on the task at hand.

Learning

The speed at which learning takes place depends somewhat upon the conditions that surround the total experience.

Time is necessary to build new movement patterns into well-controlled, semiautomatic skills. Be certain, therefore, to have patience with yourself and not to expect too much too soon. Reasonable goals should be set up and your progress toward attaining them should be reevaluated periodically.

The perfection of performance, as well as basic learning, can be speeded up if you will give complete *attention* to what you are doing at all stages of development. Work toward as accurate a performance as possible, but *do not be afraid to make mistakes.* These are a natural part of the learning process. To pressure oneself because unintentional errors occur causes undue tension and may lessen the ability to function properly. The important thing is to *identify* errors early so they do not become part of a learned pattern. Since it is not always possible to recognize one's own errors or know how to correct them, it is also necessary to *be open to the suggestions and coaching* of a knowledgeable instructor.

Work to *understand the reasons* behind the methods of executing skills and game strategies that are explained to you. This single suggestion will possibly speed up your game performance more than any other given in this chapter. Quick reaction in the game is necessary, especially in determining the appropriate means of taking advantage of openings and opportunities. When a rationale for action has been determined and is in mind, choices are much more easily made.

Changing Performance

Changing the performance of a skill that has been learned already is a special learning circumstance. It is important to understand that to completely relearn a skill in a new form will take time and will initially result in a loss of performance. If the change is one you really want to accomplish and you are willing to work hard on it, the time will be well spent. Minor adjustments can be made in skill execution during the season, but major changes and complete relearning should be reserved for the off-season to avoid the frustration of the subpar performance that may temporarily result.

PHYSICAL PREPARATION FOR PLAY

In addition to the aforementioned factors surrounding learning, numerous physical factors should also be considered.

There is a need to *develop a feeling for the ball*. The hands, wrists, and forearms need strength enough to maneuver and manipulate the ball with complete control. In addition, the fingers and wrists must be free of rigidity. Practice time spent in holding, bouncing, spinning, and passing the ball in a relaxed manner will be rewarded with improved ball-handling ability.

If movement skills are to improve there is need to *develop a feeling of body freedom* on the court. The well-skilled player experiences this; the beginner very often must learn it. This freedom begins with a confidence that during fast movement and quick changes in direction one will not lose balance or fall. Proper shoes with good-gripping soles and a well-finished court surface are of primary importance in establishing this feeling. If these conditions exist, you can rely on your shoes to hold, so relax!

Body Control

Because basketball is played in limited space and the rules demand no body contact, body control will require some concentrated attention. Once a few simple principles are understood and adhered to, body movement control is relatively easy to develop.

The body should always be kept in a *position of readiness* for movement. This is done by maintaining the body weight well balanced over both feet. The muscles should be under slight tension so that when called upon for action they will respond. With this positioning, quick starts can be made easily.

Which technique permits a player to move in place while holding the ball? Can you execute this maneuver off either foot and both forward and backward?

As you *prepare to move*, either as an offensive or defensive player, keep your feet in a fairly wide stance, while keeping your weight low by flexing the knees and hips slightly.

There are two basic movement patterns in basketball. The first of these is the *running* movement. Speed and efficiency in running are vital to success in basketball. To begin to run, the weight should be transferred to the foot nearest the direction of the desired movement. As this foot receives the weight it should drive hard off the supporting surface, sending the body forcefully into the run. The nonsupporting foot then strides to catch the weight and thrusts off the surface. While running, the stride should be long with the toes pointing straight ahead. The arms and shoulders should make strong reaching movements in alternate sequence to the strides. The hips, knees, and ankles must be maintained in a limited degree of flexion to aid in stopping and change of direction, so necessary in basketball.

The second movement pattern in basketball is the *sliding* technique. This pattern is basic to moving on defense and dribbling for control. With the sliding technique, the weight begins in balance over the stance. For the slide to begin with efficiency the stance should be spread in the direction of the intended movement. To begin the movement the weight is shifted to one foot. The other foot is brought about halfway to the weight-bearing foot, and the weight is briefly transferred to the closing-step foot. The foot in the direction of the movement again reaches out and the weight is transferred to it. The slide then proceeds in a series of step-close-step movements.

For mobility you should be prepared to run forward and backward and to turn quickly to run in either direction. Sliding movements should also be possible sidewards, forward, or backward, with the stance widened in the direction of the movement and with the weight as low as possible in good balance over the stance.

Once movement has begun, the control problem is even greater. Continue to keep the weight low and the body in a semisitting position. *Stopping*, particularly after a fast, hard run, requires that you place one foot well forward in the line of direction of the movement. This forward foot acts as a brake. To complete the well-controlled stop, quickly lower the body in balance, thrusting the weight sharply back inside the width of the stance.

Changing direction while on the move should be done with the weight well controlled over the feet. To change direction, use pivoting movements over the feet, rather than crossing the feet or using small extra steps in order to turn.

The *pivot* is the only method of moving in place that is permitted while a player is holding the ball. It is done by keeping the ball of one foot in contact with the floor and rotating the body over that foot as it turns in place. Use the nonpivot foot to step in the desired direction. The pivot can be made in either a forward or backward movement.

Jumping is a vital skill in basketball. Catching passes that are off-target and securing the ball on missed shot attempts are examples of occasions that require strong jumping skills.

Whenever possible, a two-footed take-off is recommended so that you will return to the court on the spot of take-off and thus avoid falling onto opponents and teammates. In order to jump high, start the body weight low with a deep knee bend. Using a hard leg drive, swing the arms forcefully upward as the jump is completed. Returning to the court, bend the knees and ankles to absorb the force of the contact. A concentrated effort to develop proficiency in jumping will result in increased pleasure in playing, because of ensuing greater success in performance.

Conditioning

If your body is to respond at will and be prepared to meet the demands placed upon it during the basketball game, you must concentrate on *conditioning*. This includes the development of flexibility, strength, and endurance.

Flexibility is necessary in the wrist, shoulder, trunk, and hip regions also. Practice spent in leaping, jumping, moving the body quickly, and in doing stretching exercises to increase flexibility will be rewarded with the exhilaration experienced through graceful movement.

A major factor in conditioning is to develop adequate *strength* in all the muscle groups called into play while engaged in a game of basketball. The special need for hand and arm strength has already been mentioned. Shoulder strength provides the power necessary for executing longer passes and for obtaining rebounds, while leg strength is required for jumping and running.

Strength development is best accomplished by progressively increasing the workload of muscles. The increase in work can be effected either by adding to the resistance or by doing more work in less time. Some strength development can be developed while practicing basketball skills. Where real deficiencies are present, however, a carefully established, specific exercise program may be required to bring strength up to a desirable level.

Conditioning also results in the development of both muscular and cardiorespiratory *endurance*. Endurance is the ability of the bodily systems to adapt and more efficiently function in a sustained manner when greater demands are placed upon them due to increased activity. Endurance for basketball is best developed through running (with quick stops and starts), jumping, leaping, and rope skipping. Through a progressively more demanding activity program, endurance can be developed to a high degree. Start at a level that can be tolerated and then at each practice session do a little more than was done the time before. It usually takes the average college adult about three weeks of daily, progressively more demanding work to reach a good level of conditioning. Once this is attained, it can be maintained by an all-out effort at each practice session.

Warmup

Each practice period or game should be preceded by a *warmup* session. A suggested 15-to-20-minute warmup procedure includes: (1) 2 to 3 minutes of passing and dribbling; (2) 2 to 3 minutes of unhurried, relaxed shooting; (3) 5 to 7 minutes of combination running and shooting drills; and (4) 3 to 5 minutes of concentrated shooting. This warmup permits the player to review the various skills required in the game and also provides the physiological preparation needed for going into an all-out participation situation.

Practice

Repeated execution of a skill or strategy in good form and timing, with concentrated attention to the task at hand—these are the essentials for mastery of techniques, resulting in true enjoyment of the game.

Practice time should be used to the best advantage possible. The amount of time spent in practice is not nearly as important as how that time is spent. To be of greatest value, practice should be as *gamelike* as possible. Vary the practice in intensity and difficulty of skill; this will assist by freeing you from tension and overfatigue.

Shooting practice demands special attention. Difficult shots require much application, but the easier shots should not be neglected. Balance your shooting practice in terms of type of shots, distances, and angles. Above all, concentrate on the front of the rim of the basket while shooting. Practice shooting, especially free throws, after an exhaustive effort. This suggestion is made because late in the game, when fatigue is greatest, players tend to lose the concentration necessary for shooting. Practicing while fatigued will assist you in learning to deal with this situation.

Be sure to practice carefully, purposefully, and correctly.

For a team to be able to coordinate its offensive and defensive strategies requires a concentrated effort in *team practice*. Very often individual players will think that they understand the movement and timing of the plays and therefore know what is required. Then, when confronted with the game situation against a competitive opponent, the plays break down and are ineffective because individuals have forgotten when and where to go. Team play demands the same attention and repetition in practice required in attaining mastery of the individual skills.

EMOTIONAL PREPARATION FOR PLAY

An atmosphere of mutual respect and goodwill among teammates, between opponents, and toward the officials is essential in creating a competitive situation for all participants to experience the rewards available from sport.

Attitude

Each person who participates in basketball comes to the game situation from a slightly different social and emotional background. Due to this circumstance, a variety of attitudes are in evidence among players on a given team. The importance of each individual's attitude toward the team and the game cannot be overlooked. Very often attitude, all other things being equal, is the determining factor in one team winning and another losing.

Positive thinking, optimism, and confidence are necessary for success in competition. These characteristics, coupled with skill and motivation, are essential to success. Each person will vary in the degree to which each characteristic is possessed. However, these characteristics can be learned with a concerted effort. Also, one or two members of a team who possess these characteristics can elicit similar responses from teammates. Team leaders can contribute much to the group through this kind of positive influence. Successful players often program themselves through a focus upon the positive aspects of performance. Negative attitudes toward oneself or one's teammates usually result in team or individual performances failing to reach potential.

Mutual respect among teammates is another ingredient for success and enjoyment of the game. It is important that each person accept each other person for what she is and what she can do. Jealousy, envy, and egotism have no place in team sports and are often the cause of the failure of a team to develop beyond a given point.

Appreciation of the importance of each person's role on a team is also to be considered. The starting player and the substitute alike should come from the game situation with a sense of personal worth. This can be accomplished by each team member being sensitive to each other person as a individual, not merely as a player.

Sportsmanship

Sportsmanship is a term with which each athlete is familiar. For the athlete to derive maximum values from the sport experience, sportsmanship should be a major focus for each player.

The basis for sportsmanship is respect—respect for the game, one's opponent, and those who officiate. Within this context the individual and the team will attempt to play the game within the spirit, as well as the letter of the rules. Rules are made to establish a situation of equity between opponents. For one team to play within this framework and another to intentionally violate it is to violate the ethics of the situation.

Further, the true sportswoman will respect her opponent as an individual and for the quality of the effort and performance given to the competition at hand. To do less than one's best is an affront to the opponent and the unwritten contract of the competition.

Finally, the official's role is to see that the equity provided in the rules is distributed fairly to both teams. It is essential for individuals and teams to respect the role of the official and appreciate the effort given by the officials on the behalf of the competition.

Skills essential for everyone

3

Some of the skills involved in basketball are used by both the offense and defense during a game. Other skills are used specifically on offense, while still others are employed only on defense.

The first section of this chapter describes the general skills required for play; more specific offensive and defensive skills follow in that order.

BALL-HANDLING SKILLS

Since the object of the game is to put the ball through the goal, skills designed to move the ball about the court toward the goal rate special attention.

As basketball has progressed over the years, numerous techniques for ball handling have been experimented with and developed. You will find, however, that success in basketball is not so much dependent upon the variety of skills used as upon the precision with which the very basic skills are performed.

Passing

Mastery of the following passing techniques will be a first step in insuring your value to your team.

The *chest pass* (fig. 3.1) is a good starting point. Hold the ball chest high in both hands, one hand on either side, with your fingers well spread and the ball in contact with only the fingers and the fat pads at the base of the fingers, not in the palms of the hands. With your feet in a forward-stride position, rock your weight to the rear foot as you rotate the ball toward your chest with the wrists, being sure to keep your elbows comfortably at the sides of the body and about waist high.

Fig. 3.1   The Chest Pass

In one continuous motion, step onto the forward foot as your arms begin extending forward toward the target for the pass, with the wrists rotating inward and downward. Complete the pass by fully extending the arms and releasing the ball with a quick wrist snap downward and outward, so that the fingertips flip off the bottom of the ball, thus creating a slight backspin.

Double-check your form. If you have executed the pass correctly, your elbows will reach shoulder height only *after* you release the ball. If the wrist action is correct, the palms of the hands should be facing downward and only slightly rotated outward at the completion of the pass.

The chest pass, though widely employed because of the control that can be developed with it, has limitations. For most women, because of lack of arm and shoulder strength, its use is restricted to approximately 12 to 15 feet. If this pass is used at the end of a dribble or while on the move, more power can be expected as a result of the added momentum thereby made available.

The *one-hand underhand pass* (fig. 3.2) is valuable for both shorter and longer passes. It can be used as a short flip pass at very close range or as a stronger pass to cover distances upward to fifteen feet.

Again, take a forward-stride position. As you shift your weight to the rear foot, carry the ball back on the throwing side at about hip level with both hands. The throwing hand should be behind and under the ball, with the guiding hand following the ball back to about the line of the body. At

Can you execute each of the one-hand passes with your nonpreferred hand? Can you throw them accurately for a distance of 5 feet? 8 feet? 10 feet? 15 feet?

Fig. 3.2   The One-Hand Underhand Pass

this point, release the guiding hand as the ball is carried back about 12 more inches to complete the backswing.

Start the forward movement by swinging the arm in a pendular motion, accompanying this with a step to the forward foot. Release the ball just as it passes the line of the body. At very short distances you may find that the pass can be executed with only the arm movement, eliminating the need to shift your weight.

This pass should be varied with other passes, since it can easily be blocked or intercepted if your opponent can anticipate its use every time you pass. It will be valuable to learn to use this pass with your nonpreferred hand with the same proficiency with which you can perform it with your preferred hand. This advice applies to all the one-hand skills of the game.

A pass designed for use at longer distances is the *one-hand overhand pass*, or *baseball pass* (fig. 3.3). Assume the forward-stride position. As you shift the weight to the rear foot, with both hands bring the ball to about ear level

Fig. 3.3   The One-Hand Overhand Pass

on the throwing side of the body. The throwing hand should be under and behind the ball, and the elbow should be at about shoulder height. Now release the guiding hand as you carry the ball 2 to 3 more inches for an increased "windup." Start the forward movement by swinging the elbow forward and then extending the arm upward and forward, keeping the hand under the ball. Release the ball 10 to 15 inches forward of the line of the body with a wrist snap downward at the moment of release.

As with the one-hand underhand pass, this pass can be geared downward in force for use at shorter distances by cutting down the size of the motion.

The *bounce pass* (fig. 3.4) has been developed as a deceptive action in passing and adds variety to the possible choices of passes. The object of the bounce pass is to push or throw the ball sharply toward the floor so that it will rebound upward into the hands of your teammate. The angle at which the ball will rebound from the floor is equal to the angle at which it is thrown. Added backspin on the ball will increase the angle of rebound, whereas overspin will decrease the angle of rebound (fig. 3.5). You will need to experiment with bounce passes to determine where your passes will need to be placed so that your teammates will receive the ball at about waist height.

The bounce pass can be developed from either the chest pass or a one-hand sidearm variation of the underhand pass. Simply change the point of aim from the teammate to the appropriate spot on the floor.

The two-hand overhead pass has advantages and limitations. Are you familiar with both? How should you place the feet and elbows in order to protect the ball?

Fig. 3.4   The Bounce Pass

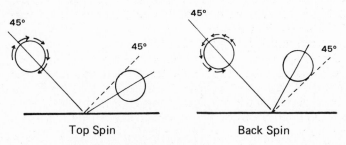

Top Spin   Back Spin

Fig. 3.5   Ball Spin and Rebound Angle

The two-hand overhead pass is used to pass for short distances over the head of one's defensive opponent. It is especially effective in directing a pass to a tall teammate who is near to, or is cutting toward, the basket. Tall players can also use this pass effectively since the ball is extended over the head and out of the reach of most opponents. Begin the pass by placing one hand on either side of the ball and bringing the ball directly over the top of the head with the elbows bent and the wrists cocked. To pass the ball, extend the elbows and snap the wrists in the direction of the desired pass. The amount of arc on the pass should be kept to a minimum, but depends a great deal on the amount of height needed to pass over the extended arms of the defensive player.

The two-hand overhead pass has limitations. The starting position keys the pass to the defense, therefore interceptions are possible. When the ball is brought overhead in a congested area the opponents can often tie up the ball. The passer should keep the elbows well out and the feet in a forward stride, thus using the body to protect the ball.

On the other hand, the two-hand overhead pass has the advantage of drawing the overeager defensive opponent into a more upright defensive stance as she reaches for the ball. If the defensive player rises up to play the ball, she is vulnerable for a drive or a pass and cut to the basket.

Aim passes between the receiver's waist and shoulders, just out of reach of her defender. It is important that your teammates be able to handle all passes with ease. It is necessary, therefore, to gauge the speed of your pass to the distance it is to cover. All passes should move quickly, but should not be thrown so hard as to be overpowering or so softly that they may be intercepted.

When passing to a teammate on the move, be sure to pass ahead of her so that she will not need to break her movement to gain possession of the ball.

In order to make really effective use of passes, vary your selection of the fundamental passes. Passing effectiveness can also be increased by learning to incorporate fake passing movements in your ball-handling skills so that your opponent may be pulled out of position on occasion.

Receiving Passes and Protecting the Ball

When receiving a pass always attempt to have full control of the ball. This can be accomplished by relaxing the arms as the ball comes into your hands and then drawing the ball in toward the body (fig. 3.6).

Your opponent is permitted to bat or snatch the ball out of your hands; therefore it is important to develop skill in protecting the ball. The most successful way of doing this is to hold the ball rather close to the body in both hands, with arms and elbows well away from the body. In this position your opponent will have difficulty getting to the ball and will be discouraged from attempting to steal it.

Once having received the pass under good control, the offensive player should assume the *ready position for offense*. Take a combination forward-side stride stance with the ankles and knees bent. The ball is held between waist and chest high with one hand on either side of the ball. From this position you are in balance to execute any one of the three movement patterns available to the offensive player: (1) shoot, (2) dribble (drive), and (3) pass (and cut).

Without looking at the ball, can you cover the length of the court with the control dribble? With either hand? Can you change hands as you go?

Fig. 3.6   Protecting the Ball

Dribbling

The *dribble* (fig. 3.7) is the technique of moving the ball to yourself by repeatedly bouncing it. The force for the first bounce may be given by one or both hands. Each subsequent bounce may be made by either hand, but only one hand may be used at a time. After the last bounce the ball may be caught in one or both hands. You are permitted only one of these dribble sequences each time you have possession of the ball.

Two types of dribbles are necessary for good ball handling. The first, the control dribble, is used to outposition your opponent and gain openings for shooting or passing. For control and change of direction the body is kept low and a low bounce is used. The ball should rebound between knee and waist height.

Take a forward-side stride stance. The foot that is forward is the one opposite the dribbling hand. This is done so that the opposite foot, arm, and shoulder will assist in protecting the ball from a defensive player who may attempt to interfere with the dribble. The movement with this dribble is done

Fig. 3.7 The Dribble

with *sliding steps* similar to those described in the next section, which discusses body control.

The hand action on the ball is one that emphasizes a pushing or pumping action of both the hand and the forearm. The fingers are spread and the ball is contacted with the fingers and the base of the fingers in the palm, avoiding contact with the full palm of the hand. Work to develop the ability to draw the ball from side to side and back and forward simply with changes in hand and wrist action.

The second dribble, *the speed dribble*, used to cover distance on the court, involves a much higher bounce than the control dribble. The ball is pushed *forward* toward the floor and should rebound between waist and chest height. Several running steps are taken during each bounce. This type of dribble is vulnerable to interception, so avoid using it while in close play with opponents.

The speed dribble is the basic technique for the fast break. As one dribbles the full length of the court at high speed several difficulties in control of the ball may occur. If the hand pushes down on top of the ball, or the ball is pushed too hard, a high bounce will result. The high bounce usually causes the player to catch the ball on the hand during the next dribble, usually an illegal dribble. This can be avoided by pushing forward on the ball and realizing that the speed of the body creates more momentum into the push than is acquired while moving more slowly, therefore, do not push as hard. Also, on the fast break, the dribbler must move at the speed at which she can

What is your point of aim when attempting a set shot from directly in front of the basket? Can you put the ball through the basket 5 times out of 10 after preceding the set shot with a dribble? 7 times out of 10?

best control the dribble or all offensive advantage is lost as a ball-handling violation is called by the official.

It is important to develop skillful use of the dribble. This requires the ability to dribble without watching the ball, as well as the ability to use either hand when executing the skill. Always use the dribble purposefully. Avoid wasting the dribble by bouncing the ball aimlessly in place.

SHOOTING SKILLS

While on offense, the player's primary function is to score goals for her team. To be effective you must develop confidence in a few fundamental shots. As accuarcy and confidence develop, you can attempt and gradually learn to master more advanced shots.

The most fundamental shot in basketball is the stationary or *set shot*. It can be used at any distance from the basket within the shooting range. The average college woman should be able to shoot the set shot up to fifteen feet or farther from the basket.

The set shot can be made with one or two hands, though the two-handed shot is more easily guarded. Since a few seconds are required to position for the two-hand shot, the one-hand set shot is recommended. This shot can be used for a free throw as well as a field goal.

One-Hand Set Shot

The following description of the *one-handed set shot* (fig. 3.8) should help in developing proficiency in the skill. It is important that each part of the description, which is written for a right-handed player, be followed carefully.

With the knees slightly bent, place the right foot ahead of the left and point the right toe directly at the center of the basket. Turn your hips and shoulders slightly so that your right side is at an angle toward the basket. With the wrist cocked back, rest the ball on the outspread fingers of the right hand, holding this position at about chin height. Support the ball with the left hand on the left side and bottom of the ball. The entire right side of the body should be aligned with the basket so that a straight line drawn through the wrist, elbow, hip, knee, and toe form a direct line to the basket. The basket is sighted over the top of the ball.

Without rocking forward or backward, begin the shot by lowering the body with a knee bend and slightly flexing the waist. Now begin to extend the legs upward and raise the upper body. Just as the legs begin to extend, straighten the elbow and raise the shoulder, pushing the ball directly upward. As the ball is pushed upward, extend the wrist upward and forward. Then

Fig. 3.8   The One-Hand Set Shot

rotate the wrist slightly outward as the ball is released from the tips of fore-finger and middle finger, causing a soft backspin.

Complete the shot by extending the total body upward, not forward. To increase the power of the shot take a deeper knee bend and push harder from the floor. Never vary the shoulder, arm, or wrist action, for to do so hampers the accuracy and "touch" of the shot.

To be an effective offensive player you must practice shooting the set shot *after a dribble*. This includes the right-handed dribble when moving to the right and the left-handed dribble when moving to the left. At the con-clusion of the dribble the body must be stopped in good balance, then the feet organized so that the shooting side is forward, toward the basket. Many shooting errors occur as a result of poor balance at the conclusion of a dribble.

It is also important to have proper balance and positioning for the set shot *upon receiving a pass.* Practice receiving passes at various angles to the basket, then shoot. Attempt to always face the basket while receiving passes so that the immediate shot for goal can be made with the minimum amount of time used for positioning.

Two-Hand Set Shot

The *two-hand set shot* is an alternate technique to the one-hand set shot. It is less desirable since the positioning for the shot takes a little longer than the one-hand shot. However, some players can develop proficiency in this technique and can use it with a degree of effectiveness.

The ball is held in front of the chest with one hand on either side of it with fingers spread. The feet are placed in a forward-stride position similar to that used in the one-hand shot. To start the shot, the body weight is lowered by bending the knees. As the legs begin to extend, both arms begin to push upward in much the same action as used in the chest pass. As the arms reach full extension the ball rolls toward the fingertips. At this point the wrists flex and rotate outward, releasing the ball with a slight backspin.

Aiming Technique

The *aiming technique* in all set shots is very similar. In general, you should attempt to drop the ball over the rim so the point of aim is the front portion of the rim. At the angles between 45 and 20 degrees on either side of the backboard it is very possible to bank the ball into the basket off the backboard. To do this, spot the point on the backboard from which the ball will carom into the basket. Remember that the ball will rebound at the same angle at which it approaches the board (fig. 3.9). This bank shot is strongly recommended for shots between these angles that are at a distance of 10 feet or shorter.

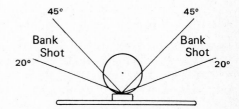

Fig. 3.9   Angles for Use of the Bank Shot

Lay-up Shot

Another fundamental type of shot is one that can be used to complete a dribble or a break toward the basket. This is called a *lay-up shot* (fig. 3.10). It is so called because the ball is softly placed against the backboard in such a manner as to cause it to rebound into the basket.

Though the shot can be executed without a dribble, it is most easily an-

Fig. 3.10   The Lay-up Shot

alyzed and practiced in conjunction with the dribble movement. The dribble used here is the one already described for covering distance.

Start on the right side of the court at about a 45 degree angle to the basket and at free throw line distance away. Push the ball toward the floor as a step is taken with the left foot, catch the ball in both hands, stride to the right foot and then to the left, leaping from the floor off the left foot, raising the right knee high so that height can be attained on the leap. As the leap is taken, carry the ball upward in front of the face with both hands, releasing the left hand and carrying the ball upward toward the backboard, with the right hand under and to the side of the ball. Release the ball without any additional throwing or pushing action. The momentum of your body transferred to the ball is enough force to carry it up to the backboard.

Can you describe two technique errors that will cause your fake to be ineffective?

The ball should be placed against the backboard just to the right of the rim edge and about 3 to 4 inches above it. This will cause the ball to rebound into the basket.

Most frequently the lay-up shot is made after driving past a defensive opponent. It is important that the nonshooting side of the body be used to protect the ball from the defensive player. The arm and shoulder, particularly, can be used to screen the opponent from the ball.

The lay-up shot can be sent from different angles to the basket. The right-handed lay-up can be shot from the left side of the basket. You can develop the skill for the left hand by reversing the footwork as described. The differing angles of approach will alter the backboard placement. Again remember, the ball will rebound at the same angle at which it is placed.

Two-Hand Overhead Shot

The *two-hand overhead shot* is a simple skill to develop and is especially useful for the tall player. This shot is very effective also for the beginning basketball player, but is used very little by the advanced player. Its use is customarily limited to a range inside of ten feet of the basket.

The overhead shot is started by holding the ball above the forehead in both hands with wrists cocked back and elbows slightly bent; the legs are bent preparatory to a push-off from the floor, similar to that employed in the one-hand set shot. The shot is executed by extending the legs, then straightening the elbows, and finally flipping the ball upward and forward with an easy wrist movement.

In order to develop accuracy and consistency in your shooting skills much careful practice is required. Always work for precision, for the smallest variation can produce errors that should not be permitted to become part of the learned movement pattern.

FAKING AND CUTTING

Faking

Faking is a skill that will become more effective as you develop ease in movement. Faking movements are used to momentarily lure your opponent out of position as she is defending so that you can more easily do what you intend to do when you are passing, shooting, or moving.

Feints may be accomplished by using the hand, the head and shoulders, the ball, the eyes, or the foot. Except for the eye fake, the body part is moved in the decoy direction, then quickly withdrawn while the true movement is

What is your present percentage of accuracy on free throws? Are you practicing the skill enough so that your ability is improving?

executed. The eye fake is effected by simply looking in one direction while you pass in another.

The head, shoulder, and foot fakes are very effective if the body maintains good balance during the fake. As the fake is made, the body weight must not overshift in the direction of the fake. If this happens all advantage gained by drawing the defensive player will be lost, since you must then have time to shift the weight back in the direction of the real movement, allowing time for the opponent to do the same. The ball should not follow the head, shoulder, or foot fake, but should be maintained in good position for the subsequent action. The ball fake is most effective when decoying a pass or a shot.

If your defensive opponent is overly eager, she may be consistently pulled out of position with fakes. For fakes to be totally effective, however, they must be realistic and convincing. Develop a variety of faking movements so that your opponent will never know what to expect. If the same fake movements are used over and over, they will lose their effectiveness; guards will learn to ignore them, knowing that they are always the same in direction or sequence.

Cutting

Cutting refers to the action of a player without the ball who moves into an open lane to receive a pass by quickly breaking around her opponent into the open. If your opponent is positioning well on defense, space may not be readily available for the cutting movement. In this case you must create space for movement by decoy actions, such as moving, then stopping quickly and cutting. Faking one direction with a foot or head and shoulder fake and then cutting in the desired direction may be effective.

Cutting is essential to good team offense. The key to its proper execution is that of moving between your opponent and the ball, thus making it difficult for her to stop the pass in to you as the cutter.

SKILLS FOR DEFENSE

The team that can neutralize the opponents' ability to score by means of a strong defense is on its way to game success. The key to a team's defense lies in the ability of each player to function on defense.

The major element in defensive technique involves *positioning*. When playing defense, take a wide forward-stride position with the weight over the balls of both feet. The ankles, knees, and hips should be flexed so that you assume a semisitting position. Keep the weight low in order to be able to move and change direction quickly. (An upright position should be used only when in close proximity to the basket.) From this stance put the hands up— one to defend the ball and the other to create an obstacle against a possible pass (fig. 3.11).

Fig. 3.11   Defensive Stance

The player-to-player defense is a basic method of team guarding. In the player-to-player system each of the five defensive players is assigned to defend against one of the opposing offensive players. In making these assignments an attempt is made to match height, speed, agility, experience and any other factors it may be necessary to consider.

Defending the Player With the Ball

When *defending against the player with the ball* establish the defensive stance between the opponent and the basket. In taking the stance the foot nearest the near sideline should be back. This stance will allow the quickest movement to cover the opponent's dribble toward the baseline (end line). The baseline drive is the most vulnerable area for defensive coverage because once the opponent dribbles past the defensive player no defensive teammates are available to help cover. The dribble toward the middle area of the court is more easily covered, since teammates of the defender are more readily available to close up open spaces for the dribble-drive.

If you are defending against a player who dribbles only to one side of the court, you can overplay one-half body width to that side to completely stifle her movement capabilities.

The distance between you and the ball handler depends upon several factors. The first factor is the distance from the basket. Since your movement actions are reactions to the offensive player's movements, you must allow for movement time and space. A second factor is a comparison of your speed in reaction and movement to that of your opponent. If you are faster than she is, you can afford to play close to her and pressure her movements. If you are slower than she is, you will need to allow more space for reaction. As you move nearer the basket, the distance between you and the ball handler should close in order to be able to stop the shot overhead.

If an opponent starts a dribble-drive it is important to stay with her on a line between her position and the basket. The movement is done with the use of sliding steps (as described in the section Body Control in chapter 2). The dribbler will usually attempt to take a circular path around you to the basket. If you were to follow her circular path it would not be possible to maintain a position between the dribbler and the basket. To maintain position it is necessary to move on a straight line to cut off the dribbler's path of movement. The objective in defending against the dribble is to force the ball handler farther away from her objective than she would like.

When defending against the player with the ball the vision is focused on the midsection of the opponent. This is the part of her body that will move if she moves. It will be easier to avoid being faked out of position with this method of vision. Avoid leaving the feet to block shots unless it is certain that the opponent's upward movement is a shot. The player who jumps up on each upward movement of the ball is easily faked out of position.

It is desirable to attempt to interfere with the dribble whenever possible. However, any reaching movement for the ball must be done while the body maintains balance and without contacting the opponent or sacrificing good footwork and movement.

Defending the Player Without the Ball

An offensive player who does not have the ball is often ignored, but this should not be the case. While *defending against the player away from the ball* you should position in a balanced defensive stance between the offensive player and the basket. The foot and hand nearest the position of the ball should be placed into the passing lane forward to your opponent. Movement is made with sliding steps. Anticipate your opponent's movements and attempt to force her away from her desired paths and cutting lanes.

Focus the vision halfway between the ball and your opponent. This will allow you to see both and make adjusting movements as necessary.

REBOUNDING

Offensive Rebounding

The team or player that can score 35 percent of the baskets attempted is considered to be successful in shooting. This means that, even when shooting well, a team needs to be concerned about regaining possession of the ball when shots are missed. *Rebounding* is the term used to describe this maneuver.

The most essential element in rebounding is positioning. In order to obtain rebound position the player who is shooting must be alert to shoot only when teammates are in advantageous rebound position. In addition, the player shooting should always follow her shot in case a rebound is necessary.

As a shot goes up to the basket, quick movement to position must be made by at least three offensive players. The most advantageous position is that of being closer to the basket than the opponent. Experience in watching the flight of the ball will assist you in knowing at what angles to anticipate rebounds on any given shot.

As the ball comes down, jump high, grasp the ball with a strong grip, and place the arms well out to protect it. Keep the ball high and immediately attempt a second shot if at all possible. If the defense has recovered and there is no opening for a second shot, look for pass opportunities to teammates who may be open to shoot. If it is not possible to grip the ball, a well-directed tap of the ball away from the basket will probably put it in a better position for your teammates to recover, since the defense will probably be in quite close to the basket. The team who controls the rebounding has a decided advantage because its members have more shooting opportunities, while at the same time limiting the opponents' chances to score.

Defensive Rebounding

Defensive players must be alert to *rebound* as many of their opponents' missed shot attempts as possible. Rebounding involves teamwork as well as indi-

Fig. 3.12   Defensive Rebounding

From the standpoint of mechanics, why is it more difficult to aim a hook shot accurately than a set shot? Have you practiced the hook shot until you can deliver it with good precision?

vidual skill. The defense, as a group, attempts to keep the offensive players away from the basket. As a shot is made, each defensive player should turn quickly and screen out her opponent by taking a broad stance, yet maintaining a position from which she can jump (fig. 3.12). If each player has been positioning properly and then positions for rebounding, the result will be a fine team effort.

It is necessary to jump high for the ball, placing the hands around it with the arms well out to the sides for ball protection. As you return to the court, bring the ball to about waist height, protecting it all the while with your arms. As soon as you have regained a position on the court, look for an opening and pass quickly to a teammate. If this is not possible, dribble diagonally toward the nearest sideline and centerline.

If you practice and give careful attention to the individual skills of basketball, you will soon be able to integrate them into effective team play.

Better players master these techniques

4

The ease with which the well-skilled basketball player moves and performs is a pleasure to behold. Careful scrutiny will disclose that for the most part this person performs all of the fundamental skills discussed in the last chapter, but does so with a higher degree of accuracy and ease than the novice.

It will be noticed also that the better player usually has incorporated some additional individualized skills into her repertoire. Some of these can be used by any player on the court. Others are limited to a player in a specific position or to players with special capabilities.

The offensive player is afforded many more opportunities for variety in skills than is the defensive player. The latter must be content to counteract the opponent's maneuvers in the best possible manner. This leaves very little room for creativity or novelty of action, but provides much opportunity for quick perception, rapid decision making, and effective action.

ADVANCED SHOOTING TECHNIQUES

Jump Shot

The most commonly observed advanced shooting technique is the *jump shot* (fig. 4.1). In this shot the player delays the release of the ball until she has jumped high into the air, thus shooting over the top of her opponent's hands. It is extremely difficult to defend.

The jump shot is in actuality very similar to the one-hand set shot described earlier. The body position and alignment are identical for both shots, but they do differ in timing, in the starting position, and in the release of the ball. Rather than starting the ball at chest height, as in the one-hand set shot, the ball rests in the shooting hand at a position just above the fore-

Fig. 4.1   The Jump Shot

head, supported on one side by the nonshooting hand. The basket is sighted under the ball with each eye looking past its repective side of the wrist.

With the ball in front of the chest, the preparation for the jump begins with a deep knee bend. Then pushing off the floor with a hard thrust upward, the ball is brought to shooting position as the body is extended into the air. At the very top of the jump the shooter relaxes and pushes the ball softly upward and slightly forward with the same action as that used in the one-hand set shot.

The stationary shot described is used within 3 to 10 feet of the basket. Since at greater distances the shooter usually needs more momentum than can be developed in the stationary jump shot she shoots after having dribbled or bounced the ball, taking a two-step approach in the jump.

The timing of the shot after the dribble differs slightly from that in the stationary shot. The shooter bounces, then takes two steps into a deep knee bend as the ball is caught, making sure the shooting side of the body is slightly forward and aligned with the basket. The ball is then carried up to the position as the jump is made. Care is taken to jump upward and not forward to avoid contacting the defender.

The mechanics of the jump shot can also be converted into a *jump pass*. The only difference is in the direction of the release. Since the opponents do not know whether to anticipate a shot or a pass, the addition of the jump pass to your repertoire creates added deception as well as mobility.

Hook Shot

In some types of team organization one or two players are called upon to play with their backs to the basket some of the time. From this position it is necessary to develop appropriate additional shooting techniques. One of these is the *hook shot* (fig. 4.2). This shot is particularly effective when performed by a tall player, but even the player of average height finds that the hook shot is almost impossible for her opponents to guard. Performed anywhere from close range to distances of 10 to 15 feet from the basket, the hook shot is one of the most breathtaking, spectacular shots in the game.

Fig. 4.2   The Hook Shot

Starting with the back to the basket, the right-handed player begins by pivoting on the left foot, thus bringing the left shoulder toward the basket as the ball is raised in both hands from the right hip to about shoulder height. At this point the left hand leaves the ball as the right arm extends outward with the ball balanced in the palm of the hand. As the full pivot is completed, the arm lifts directly overhead in a circular motion, with the ball being released off the fingertips when it is approximately over the right shoulder.

Opportunities to employ the hook shot may come after a bounce or dribble across the front of the basket. A player may also develop the ability to cut into an opening in front of the basket, receive a pass, and send the ball to the basket with a hook shot. The beauty of the shot lies not only in the graceful flow of movement but in the veritable impossibility of defending against it.

As with the jump pass, the hook shot has its counterpart in the *hook pass*. This pass is valuable for getting rid of the ball when in close quarters and for passing over the top of a tall opponent. When accompanied with a jump, the possibilities for getting off a hook pass increase still more.

Turnaround Shot

The *turnaround shot* is a combination of movements in which a player with her back to the basket makes a quick pivot in place and shoots. The turnaround can be combined with the one-hand set shot, the jump shot, or the two-hand overhead shot. An advanced player can develop one or more of these shots to a high degree of proficiency and then may add to her general effectiveness through the ability to pivot both left and right. The difficulty in the turnaround shot lies in the fact that the shooter has only a moment in which to sight the basket before releasing the ball. When combined with faking movements and good jumping ability, however, the turnaround shot is very difficult to guard, especially in close range of the basket.

Fall-Away Shot

The *fall-away shot* is another maneuver that is not really a specific shot, but a combination of movements. The fall-away can be combined with almost any shot, including the turnaround. The performer simply leans away from her defender and the basket as the shot is released, continuing in that direction during the follow-through. Again, this shot is difficult to guard. The major disadvantage of this shot is that its shooter can almost be discounted as a rebounder, since she is moving away from the basket and consequently is usually off balance.

The average basketball player is amazed at the ability of some of the better players to put spin on the ball when shooting, thus causing it to rebound at almost impossible angles off the backboard and into the basket. Along with this, the advanced performer has developed the ability to execute lay-up shots from any angle on the court. Even having passed under the basket, by reversing the shot from the far side in an over-the-head release, such a player can shoot for a basket. These skills all take hours of practice to develop and you will observe that even the skillful player uses these "fancy shots" only on rare, but opportune, occasions.

DRIBBLING TACTICS

Effective ball-handling tactics of the skilled basketball player are necessary to enhance the other movement aspects of the game. Strong *dribbling tactics* are designed to give the player better mobility and give her an opportunity to place the defensive player in an off-balance position. Ball-handling tactics are especially necessary for the offensive player who brings the ball up court when moving from the defensive end of the offensive frontcourt. Often the opponents will pressure the ball handler. If this defense is of a player-to-player variety, either one of the following tactics can be employed. Both tactics can also be employed by the skilled offensive player to gain openings for shot attempts in conjunction with the jump shot.

The *crossover dribble* (fig. 4.3) is used when moving under a moderate amount of defensive pressure. As the dribbler moves up court she dribbles toward one side of the floor, using the hand on that side as the dribbling hand. If the defensive player does not follow her path to cut it off, the dribbler has used the movement angle to gain passage into the front court. If the defensive player moves to cut off the diagonal movement, the dribbler simply pulls the ball across the body toward the other hand and dribbles at an opposite diagonal pathway into the front court. If the defensive player is within arm's reach of the ball, a very low bounce is used on the crossover movement.

A *reverse dribble* (fig. 4.4) is an effective dribbling tactic when under heavy defensive pressure. As the defensive player closes in, the dribbler places the nondribbling hand, shoulder, and foot between the defensive player and the ball and pivots, thus turning her back on the defensive player. The dribbler then turns, changes hands on the dribble, and drives to the side opposite to that of the original movement.

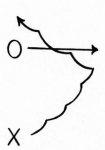

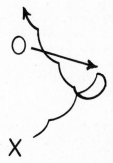

Fig. 4.3   The Crossover Dribble   Fig. 4.4   The Reverse Dribble

What is the most important element in the performance of the tip-in? Have you perfected this skill or would you be better advised to use a standard offensive rebound?

TIP-IN

The *tip-in* (fig. 4.5) is a difficult skill for most girls and women to develop. It involves jumping to meet a rebound, catching the ball momentarily in mid-air, and then pushing it into a return shot, all before returning to the court. Though the tip-in requires a strong hand and arm, the most important aspect of this skill is the timing of the jump. A player who can accomplish a good tip-in is valuable to her team. If she is inconsistent, however, a standard offensive rebound is preferable, for it more nearly insures possession of the ball.

Fig. 4.5   The Tip-in

DEFENSIVE ACTION

Defensive as well as offensive players in advanced level play need to know offensive techniques. In order to anticipate what an opponent will do the defensive player looks for clues in the offensive player's movements. By knowing what is necessary in order to execute an opponent's favorite skill the defender can position herself so that she can stifle or alter the offensive player's preparatory movements. The defensive player should always attempt to force the opponent into a *less choice option* than the one she had planned. Occasionally, therefore, a player may guard her opponent to the side to restrict her movement in her favorite direction or guard her from the side or front to keep the ball from being passed to a player who can shoot hook shots effectively. These are but a few methods of positioning that enhance the guards' chances of restricting the well-skilled offensive player in an effective manner.

Additionally, a good defensive player works constantly to gain rebounds, and almost as soon as she has possession of the ball, attempts to clear the ball quickly to a teammate who should be breaking toward her own goal.

As a performer you may wish to experiment with some of these skills. As a spectator you will certainly learn to appreciate the practice, patience, and concentration that have gone into the skillful player's development.

Basic concepts for offensive and defensive action

5

The concept of strategy is basic to all sports, but in no sport can strategy remain more simple or become more intricate than in basketball. The game is a constant attempt to force the opponent into a position where the balance between offense and defense is lost and then to quickly take advantage of the situation. This game of wits is fun and exciting, but requires full command of the basic skills and a thorough knowledge of the patterns of team play to be used.

The basketball team consists of five players who function together for a coordinated effort. Often, however, the team patterns are dependent upon the individual player execution of movements or the coordinated movement of two or three teammates at a time. Basic concepts of strategy and one-, two- or three-player tactics will precede a discussion of team play for five players.

The various strategies of basketball are built on a few simple concepts. These fundamental concepts are presented so that the discussion of the specific aspects of strategy will have more meaning.

First of all, all offensive and defensive systems are predicated upon the ability of the team members to *accurately execute the fundamentals* of passing, dribbling, shooting, and moving with good body control. The most carefully devised system will be impossible to carry out if fundamental skills are weak. If a given team system does not work, it is important to evaluate this aspect before changing the system. When selecting offensive or defensive systems it is necessary to consider whether the individual players on the team possess the skills demanded for executing a given system.

Secondly, the concept of *shooting percentages* must be considered. The nearer to the basket the shooter is, the greater are the chances that she will score a given shot. Conversely, the farther away the shooter is from the basket, the greater are the chances that she will miss a given shot. The potential *shooting range of the offense dictates the defensive action.* If the offensive team can shoot a high percentage of shots to an extended range the defensive team must challenge the offense to that range, leaving more space for cuts to the basket. If the offensive team is not capable of scoring longer shots, the defensive team can play nearer the basket, inviting the potentially inaccurate long shot and covering the cutting lanes to the basket.

Thirdly, the *offensive choice of action is dependent upon the defensive action.* If the defense challenges the offense away from the basket, the offensive choice should be to cut or drive around the defense to the basket. If the defense sags toward the basket, the offense should work to gain close-range outside shots.

Finally, *every defense has a vulnerability and every offense has a lesser choice of action.* The vulnerability that a strong defense will expose to the offense will be the one least available to or desirable by the offense. The defense should take away what the opposing offense can most frequently and effectively accomplish; the defense should give away what the offense is least able to do or less likely to locate. On the other hand, the offense seeks out the vulnerability of the defense in order to capitalize on it.

The following sections should be read with concepts in mind. If you become a *thinking* basketball player you will not only become more successful, but you will gain more of the thrills that the game can afford.

Patterns of offensive play

6

ONE-ON-ONE TACTICS

Player with the Ball

Before team offense can be generated, individual player movement must be developed. As the *player with the ball*, be prepared to take advantage of the defense whenever possible. If the defensive player sags toward the basket, you should shoot over her; if the defensive player challenges you or uses poor defensive movement, fake her out of position and drive (dribble) for a lay-up. Among the errors you can learn to watch for, and consequently take advantage of, are: standing too erectly; overshifting the weight to one foot while moving; leaving the feet in attempting to block shots; overanxiously reacting to fake movements; crossing the feet when changing direction; putting the weight on the heels when standing still or stopping; and bringing the body too close to the offensive player outside a radius of about 18 feet from the basket.

By developing strong offensive abilities you will be able to keep your opponent off balance because she will never know quite what to anticipate with regard to your next action.

Try to position with the ball in the ready position for offense, facing the basket. It is important to focus the vision toward the center of the court so that opportunities for passes to teammates can be seen or that openings for individual offensive actions can be anticipated.

The *fake and drive* (fig. 6.1) is basic to sound one-on-one tactics. The dribbling movement for the lay-up shot is called a *drive* for the basket. The ability to drive around an opponent can be developed by a careful study of the guarding techniques of opponents.

Can you name defensive player errors that the player with the ball can use to her advantage?

Fig. 6.1   The Fake and Drive

The key to being able to drive around your opponent without contact is good footwork. The footwork for the drive to the right is begun with a foot fake to the left with the left foot. The next move is to quickly take a crossover step with the left foot as the ball is pushed into the dribble with the right hand. If this left foot can be placed just outside the left foot of the defender, do not hesitate to continue around her because you now have the right-of-way to the basket. A drive to the left is done by reversing all of the foregoing directions.

Key to Diagrams:

X   Offense

✳   Player with Ball

O   Defense

⟶   Player

⟿   Dribble

---→   Pass

Player Without the Ball

The offensive movement of the *player without the ball* is very important to successful team offense. It is necessary, when not in possession of the ball, to constantly keep the defensive players concerned about you by faking cuts or by moving in such a way as to set up your teammates' actions. This will be more clearly described in the following sections.

Very often the defensive players will position so that the passing lane to you from the ball handler is closely guarded. When this is the case, it is necessary to make yourself *available to receive a pass*. This is most easily accomplished by a tactic called the *jam and release*, or diagonal reverse (fig. 6.2). If the defensive player is playing partially between you and the ball, take one or two quick steps in the direction away from the ball. Usually the defensive player will follow you. As she does, quickly stop (jam) with a braking step, turn, and move toward the pass (release). Upon receiving the pass, pivot and face the basket to function as the player with the ball, looking for opportunities to drive, pass, or shoot. If the defensive player does not follow your movement away from the ball, you should make a cut behind her toward the basket.

Fig. 6.2   The Jam and **Release**

TWO-PLAYER PATTERNS

The team patterns of basketball offense can be defined as variations of some basic models that can be most easily worked between two players. These are the cut-ins, the give and go, and the various forms of the screen and roll. To develop five-player patterns is to develop sequences, options, and combinations of the basic two-player patterns.

Front Door Cut

The simplest of the patterns is the front door cut (fig. 6.3). In this pattern a player without the ball fakes her defensive opponent out of position and cuts

Have you practiced the give and go until you can easily perform it with a front door cut, a back door cut, and a split cut?

to the basket as the teammate with the ball times a pass to the cutter at the first moment she is free, with the pass leading the cutter toward the basket.

Fig. 6.3   The Front Door Cut

Since space is necessary in order for this pattern to develop, it is usually best executed when the defensive opponent defends at a distance away from the basket. The direction of the cut depends on the defender's starting position. If the defensive player plays straightaway to the basket, the fake is made away from the ball with the subsequent cut being made between the defender and the ball. The footwork for the front door cut is shown in figure 6.3.

Back Door Cut

If the defense player overplays to the side of the ball a back door cut is used. This is accomplished with a fake toward the ball, then a cut behind the defender to the basket. The footwork for this is shown in figure 6.4. The back

Fig. 6.4   The Back Door Cut

door cut can also be used when the defensive player does not take the fake when attempting to set up the front door cut.

Give and Go

The *give and go* is a passing maneuver basic to many ball-type games. Player A passes to player B. Player A then makes a fake and a cutting movement to a more advantageous position and receives a return pass. The pass is the "give"; the cutting movement is the "go." The cut used can be a front door or a back door cut, as described above. The cut can also be a *split cut*. In this maneuver the cutter moves around the person to whom she passed, thus inhibiting her defender in following the cut. This can be seen in the diagram in figure 6.5.

Screen and Roll

The *screen and roll* has a number of purposes and a wide number of variations. The simplest form of the screen is the shooting screen, a technique in which one player places her body between her teammate and that player's defender, thus leaving the teammate in a momentarily unguarded position to shoot. There are several methods of establishing the shooting screen (fig. 6.6).

The first method is possible only against a passive defense. In it, the ball handler passes to a teammate and then follows the pass to place herself as a screen in front of the teammate's defender. The second method is more easily accomplished and calls for player A to pass to player B. Then A follows the pass toward B and moves outside B's position so that B becomes the screen. Player B then pivots and passes to A, who shoots. A third method of screening is accomplished as player A establishes a stationary position on the court. Player B then uses basic one-on-one faking tactics to lose her defensive player and moves into a shooting position using A as a screen.

Once the screened position is established, often the defender, who is screened out, will slip around the screen. If this happens, the screener should pivot toward the basket in the direction from which the defender has come, moving to the basket to receive a pass. This is called a *roll* movement (fig. 6.8).

Pick-off Screen and Roll
The *pick-off* screen is a more advanced technique in screening. It is a triple-threat tactic in which the screen provides the options of (1) a drive, (2) a roll, and (3) a shot, depending on the defensive adjust-

Fig. 6.5   The Give and Go—Split Cut

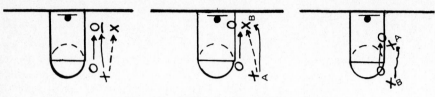

Fig. 6.6   Methods of Establishing Screens

Fig. 6.7   The Screened Shot

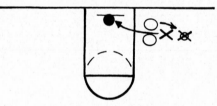

Fig. 6.8   The Screen and Roll

ments. Player A passes to B and then moves into a screen position, as in the first screen described. Instead of moving in front of B's opponent, however, A moves to the side of that player. A's defender follows her and waits to see what will happen. Player B, now with the ball, remains stationary until the screen, or pickoff, has been set. She then begins to dribble toward the side on which the screen has been set. Her defender cannot follow her since she has been screened out of the movement. Player B may be able to go all the way in to shoot (fig. 6.9). If, however, A's original opponent is alert, she will switch positions and move in to guard B when she sees her teammate cannot follow. This brings in the option, *the roll* (fig. 6.10).

As A's opponent switches, A, using a rear pivot, pivots toward the basket, and B, seeing she is now covered, passes to A, who is unguarded and may shoot. Timing for the pick-off and roll is crucial. The screener must be stationary before the drive starts, for the screener will be called for a blocking foul should contact with the defensive opponent occur. In addition, the roll and the pass to her must occur at the very instant that the blocker's defender switches in order to insure that the play will work.

An additional option is available to the skilled player. If B, while beginning the drive, sees she can use the screen for a screened shot, she stops for a jump shot over the shoulder of the screener.

Fig. 6.9   The Pick-off and Roll—Drive Option

Fig. 6.10   The Pick-off and Roll—Roll Option

THREE-PLAYER PATTERNS

Double Split

In several instances the features of the two-player patterns can be utilized by three players. Among the many three-player patterns are (1) the double split and (2) the pick-off screen away from the ball.

The *double split* (fig. 6.11) is an extension of the *give and go*. A player (the pivot player) takes a position with her back to the basket. Two of her teammates are spaced opposite her, facing the basket, so that the three players form a triangle of position. Either player facing the basket starts with the ball and passes it to the pivot player. The passer fakes to one side and then executes a split cut around the pivot player. In the meantime the nonpassing cutter also fakes away and then executes a second split cut around the pivot

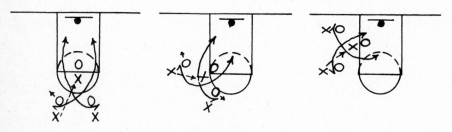

Fig. 6.11   The Double Split of the High Post

player. The pivot player can choose to pass to either cutter. If neither appears to be open, the pivot player raises the ball overhead and pivots toward the basket. From here the pivot player looks for an open shot, her own drive to the basket, or a delayed pass to either cutter. Timing and space are important in this tactic. Remember, the passer gets the first cut.

Pick-off Away from the Ball

The *pick-off away from the ball* (fig. 6.12) has many uses in a five-player offense. It requires that the ball handler be alert to pass to a cutting teammate. The pattern begins as one offensive player, A, gets a pick-off screen to the side of the defensive opponent of a teammate who does not have the ball. As soon as the screen is stationary, B cuts around the side of the screen and looks for a pass from the passer, C. B's defender is unable to follow her assigned opponent, so if A's defender is not alert to switch and cover B, B will be open to go to the basket to score.

All the intricate plays possible in basketball can be developed from the one-on-one tactics and the three- and two-player patterns. This can be shown in the following section, which is devoted to the team offense.

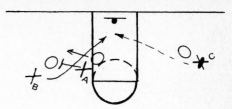

Fig. 6.12   Pick-off Away from the Ball

ORGANIZING THE OFFENSE

When five players are assembled in the offensive end of the floor it is necessary to establish a basic organization to avoid confusion in positioning and movement and to insure adequate scoring opportunities.

The basis of each offensive system of organization is *floor position*.

Single-Post Offense

The *single-post offense* is the system most commonly used. In this system the five players are positioned as indicated in figure 6.13.

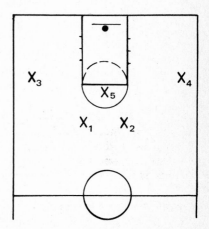

Fig. 6.13   Floor Position—Single-Post Offense

Players X1 and X2 are positioned in the backcourt area and are called *guards*. They are spaced no farther apart than the distance at which they can effectively pass to one another (usually 15-18 feet), and set up well outside the top of the key area. The guards should possess good ball-handling and movement abilities, since they most often bring the ball up the floor from the defensive end and also initiate the offensive action with passes and cutting movements.

Players X3 and X4 are the *forwards*. Forwards should be the team's taller players who can shoot well facing the basket and should also possess the ability to cut to the basket. The forwards should begin 3-4 feet from the side-line at a position approximately opposite the free throw line.

The fifth team member is usually called the *center* and positions with her back to the basket somewhere near the free throw lane (X5). This player is usually the tallest team member and capable of shooting hook shots or turn-around shots. The center is also known as the *post* or *pivot player*. When she positions within an 8 to 10 foot radius to the basket, she is called a *low post*. As the low post her primary consideration, upon receiving a pass, is to turn and shoot. Her secondary consideration is to hand off passes to teammates and to screen for them. When the post player positions at a 12 to 18 foot radius to the basket she is called a *high post*. The high post's primary consideration, upon receiving a pass, is to pass off to teammates, who will make cuts to the basket; her secondary consideration is to turn and drive to the basket or shoot.

From the basic floor position the guards and forwards can move in a choice of cutting pathways as shown in figure 6.14. The post player moves around and across the lane as shown in figure 6.15.

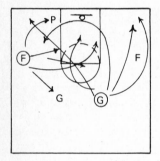

Fig. 6.14   Potential Movement Path of a Guard and a Forward

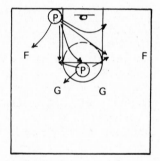

Fig. 6.15   Potential Movement of a Post Player

Double-Post—Tandem Post
Figures 6.16 and 6.17 give two alternate floor positions, the *double post* and the *tandem post*. In each of these, X1 functions as a guard, while X2 and X3 function as forwards and may, on occasion, function as guards. The players X4 and X5 are post players. In the double post either post player can alternate into high or low post positions. In the tandem post X4 and X5 function as high and low post, respectively.

Organization—Movement
There are two methods of organizing the offense—patterned offense and free-lance offense. The *patterned offense* is designed so that the team has a series of player movements, therefore shot possibilities or *options* occur in sequence. Defensive counters are anticipated to each movement, allowing alternate

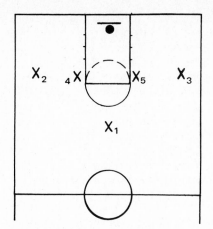

Fig. 6.16 Floor Position—Double-Post Offense

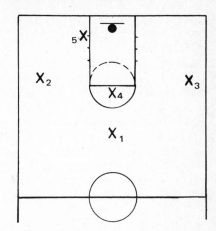

Fig. 6.17 Floor Position—Tandem-Post Offense

choices of action to be preplanned. If one option is not available the pattern moves to the next option in sequence. When all options have been used, players have a preplanned movement that will bring the team back to the original floor position, and the pattern can be started again. If the pattern sequences bring the players automatically back to the original floor position, the pattern is called a *continuity*. If some adjustment of rebalance is necessary after the last option, the pattern is called a *semicontinuity*. Patterns are keyed by a word cue, hand signal, or the movement pathway of one of the guards. All players should be alert to "read" the keying movements and to see opportunities for certain options.

The *free-lance* offense is one in which the team plays without prescribed sequences of movement. Two or three players at a time work any of the two- or three-player patterns. This type of offense is usually more difficult to organize than the patterned offense, since all the players must be alert to know another's movements and to see the openings for given patterns. Beginners tend to have difficulty with the free-lance offense due to confusion and lack of experience and often fail to recognize the opportunities to use certain choices of attack.

OFFENSE—ATTACKING THE PLAYER-TO-PLAYER DEFENSE

The offense against a player-to-player defense should be quick to take position and to initiate movements. Movement is essential to keep the opponents off balance. Floor position is necessary to gain adequate spacing for the cutting patterns basic to the player-to-player offense. Most patterns begin with either a guard-to-forward pass, a guard-to-guard pass, or a guard-to-post pass. This is called the "lead" pass for the pattern and usually keys the start of the offense. The player who receives the lead pass must fake effectively to free herself to receive the pass (jam and release). The post player, especially, must avoid standing in one position and must fake to gain the proper position for the pattern.

Once the offensive pattern begins, *players away from the ball must make faking movements* without getting in the way of the primary option, while maintaining timing to set up secondary options. If these types of movements away from the ball are not executed, the defenders away from the ball can drift into the lane area, away from their assignments, and double-cover the open players who have worked very hard to gain the advantage.

Finally, most offensive patterns are designed to place one player, usually a guard but sometimes a forward, in the backcourt for *defensive balance*. This is done so that if the defense intercepts a pass or rebounds a missed shot, the offense will have at least one player to drop back quickly and defend against a fast break.

Single-Post Offense

The following sections outline several semicontinuity patterns that utilize the single-post system and can be employed against a player-to-player defense.

In figure 6.18 three options are outlined for a single pattern.

a. As G2 passes to F4, G1 fakes left and uses C5 as screen for a "split" cut without the ball. If G1 gets free, F4 passes to her for an easy lay-up shot. If G1 receives the pass and C5's defender switches to cover, C5 should move to the basket for a pass from G1. If F4 does not pass to G1, G1 clears through the lane to the opposite side, while C5 moves to a high post position on the side of the lane.

b. Option II is established as a "double split." F4 passes to C5. F4 and G2 split the post. As G1 sees the pass to the post, she comes back into the backcourt for defensive balance.

c. Option III is an alternate to option II. If F4 chooses not to pass to C5, then C5 sets a pick-off screen on F4's defender. C5 and F4 can play "pick and roll." Meanwhile, when G1 sees that the pass did not go to the post for option II, she sets a pick-off screen for F3, who can cut to the basket and receive a pass from F4 if the pick-off and roll with C5 does not transpire.

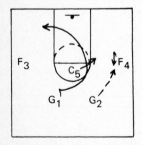 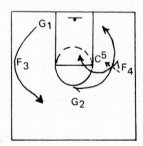 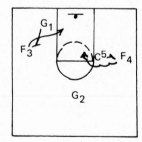

Fig. 6.18   Single-Post Pattern—Guard Through

The pattern shown in figure 6.19 utilizes a double screen.

a. G2 passes to F4 and executes any one of three cutting options: she can fake and execute a front door cut to the basket; she can set a pick-off screen for F4 and they can do a pick-off and roll sequence; or she can do a "split" cut outside of F4. Meanwhile, C5 and F3 form a double screen at the left side of the lane.

b. If no opening is gained in option I, G2 cuts around the double screen as F4 passes to G1, who can either do a one-on-one drive or pass to G2, who has a screened shot.

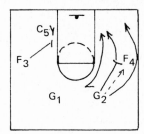 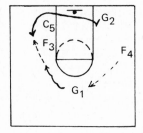

Fig. 6.19   Single-Post Pattern—Double Screen

In figure 6.20 G2 passes to F4 and sets a pick-off screen. G2 and F4 can do a pick-off and roll sequence. Meanwhile, C5 sets a pick-off screen for F3, who cuts to the basket.

The pattern in figure 6.21 utilizes the double split. G1 passes to C5 and does a split cut. G2 follows with another split cut. If neither G1 or G2 is open for a handoff pass from C5, C5 turns to the basket and looks for a secondary opening. If neither guard is immediately open under the basket, they clear out outside the forwards, who are faking to set up a cut to the basket. C5 can pass to a forward cutting or can drive for her own shot.

The patterns above are a sample of the many that can be devised using the cuts, give and go, and screen patterns described at the beginning of this chapter. You are directed to the bibliography at the end of this section for books that will give additional patterns for offense against the player-to-player defense.

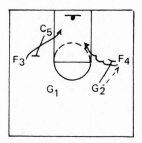 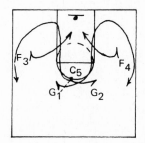

Fig. 6.20   Single-Post Pattern—Pick-off Away from the Ball

Fig. 6.21   Single-Post Pattern—Double Split

Can you devise three original patterns using cuts, give and go, and screens and then plan the cues for each pattern?

OFFENSE—ATTACKING THE ZONE DEFENSE

The zone defense is designed to place players into areas surrounding the basket so that the high-percentage scoring areas are well-covered. Several basic factors are necessary to create openings for medium- to short-range shots.

The first factor in attacking the zone defense is to *place the offensive players in the seams of the zone coverage.* The seams are the points of the zone at which the defenders will shift responsibilities to or away from the ball. Positioning in the areas between defensive deployment may create momentary hesitation between the two players for the coverage of the ball. Figure 6.22 illustrates the various vulnerable zone areas of the 2-3, 2-1-2, and 1-2-2 zones.

Another objective in playing against the zone should be to *spread the zone coverage* so that openings for cuts to the basket or short-range shots may be obtained. The most effective means of spreading the zone is to establish the fact that the offense can *score long-range shots.* This will force the defense to actively guard the ball at a greater distance from the basket than normal. In addition, the player in possession of the ball can draw the defense to her by faking a shot or dribbling directly at the point between two defenders. By drawing the defense out with either the shot or the dribble, openings are created behind the defenders for cutters to make movements to the basket.

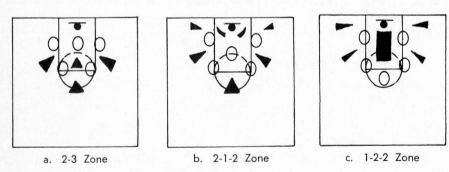

a. 2-3 Zone   b. 2-1-2 Zone   c. 1-2-2 Zone

Fig. 6.22   Areas of Zone Vulnerability

A third tactic to gain short-range shots is to run *cutters through the zone* so that either the cutter will be available to receive a pass or defenders will collapse to cover the cutter, making medium-range shots possible from the outside. Cutters should work to cut to the vulnerable spots inside the zone so that defensive players must move to cover the cut.

It is essential, while attacking the zone, to *pass the ball quickly* and to *avoid the use of the dribble*. Dribbling should only be done when moving in a purposeful manner. Dribbling in place or at random will simply allow the defense to stabilize position. Fast passing will force the defense to move to cover the movement of the ball, thus creating the possibility that some coverage will be slow to take effect. The alert offense will take advantage of poor movement.

The zone can be weakened by *overloading a zone*. This is done by placing two offensive players for one defender to cover, or three offensive players for two defenders to cover. Most of the patterns shown below establish a series of overloads.

The final method of attack is that of *playing the weak side* of the zone. This refers to playing the ball to one side of the floor, thus drawing the zone coverage to that side of the floor. A pass is quickly made to the other side of the floor for an open shot before the defense can recover. *Screening* for a shot can be done on the weak side. As the zone is pulled to one side of the floor an offensive player establishes a screen in the potential path of a defensive player. As the ball is moved toward the screener's side of the floor the defensive player is inhibited from moving, thus creating a screen for a medium-range shot. The screen and roll tactic can be used in this situation. The screen to the weak side can be seen in figure 6.24.

The various zone patterns shown below attempt to take advantage of the concepts of attacking the zone presented above. The single-post, double-post, and tandem-post systems are shown.

Single-Post Offense

Figure 6.23 outlines a pattern where a guard cuts to the baseline.

a. As G2 passes to F4, G1 cuts to the baseline on the ball side of the floor. After the guard cuts, C5 moves to the side of the lane. This maneuver should create an overload.

b. F4 has the option of shooting or passing to either C5 or G1. Often a pass to either of these players will free the other for a shot. For example, a

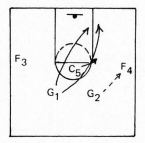 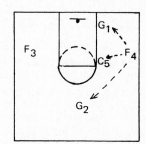 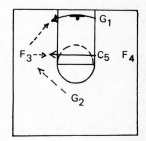

Fig. 6.23   Single-Post Zone Offense—Guard to Baseline

pass from F4 to C5 may shift the zone so that G1 will be open to receive a pass from C5. If no shot is available, the ball is passed to G2 at the top of the key.

c. G2 passes to the weak side to F3. F3 can shoot or pass to cutters C5 and G1. Both cutters should cut to the open areas of the zone. If a pass goes to either cutter, the zone may shift and create an opening for a pass to F3 for an unguarded shot. This pattern can be used back and forth from one side of the floor to the other. G2 should look for a shot from the top of the key if the defense sags to cover the cutters or the weak side.

In figure 6.24 a screen is set up on the weak side of the zone.

a. This sequence shows the weak-side screen. G2 passes to F4 and cuts to the baseline. C5 moves to the side of the lane. Any of the overload opportunities can be used. Meanwhile, F3 moves to set a screen on the weak-side baseline defender.

b. If the ball is passed to the weak side, G2 moves around the screen to receive the pass. It is usually necessary for G1 to dribble the ball toward the weak side of the floor to gain a good passing lane. C5 moves to a high post position to draw the defense high, allowing an opening for the roll off the screen.

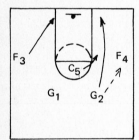 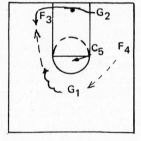

Fig. 6.24 Single-Post Zone Offense—Weak-Side Screen

The play pattern shown in figure 6.25 depends on a continuity in cutting.

a. As G2 passes to F4, C5 moves to the high side post position. G2 cuts to the baseline position. This positioning usually creates an overload situation. If shot is not open, the sequence moves to b.

b. If no opening occurs F4 passes to G1 who has centered on the floor.

c. As G1 passes to the weak side, to F3, C5 cuts across the lane in the high post area. F4 makes a delayed cut to the opening behind C5 and moves to the baseline on the opposite side of the floor. G2 moves to the space vacated by F4. F3 looks for any overload opportunity available.

d. If no shot occurs, F3 passes to G1, who passes to G2. Meanwhile, C5 cuts through the high post area, and F3 cuts to the opening behind C5 to the baseline. Again, G2 looks for overload opportunities. F4 moves to the spot vacated by F3. This pattern is a continuity.

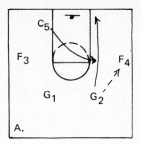

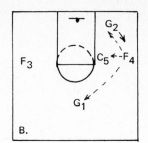

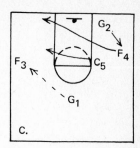

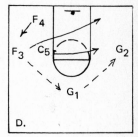

Fig. 6.25   Single-Post Zone Offense—Cutting Continuity

Double Post—Tandem Post

Figure 6.26 illustrates the double post zone offense.

a. As G1 passes to F3, P5 moves to the baseline and P4 cuts across the lane.

b. If F3 can find no overload opportunities, she passes to G1.

c. As G1 passes to F2, P4 cuts across the high post area and then slides down toward the baseline in the low post area. P5 makes a delayed cut behind P4 to the high post area. This pattern can be reversed to the other side of the lane.

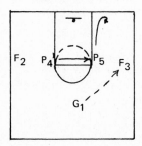

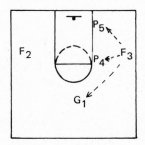

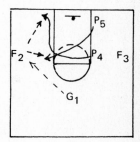

Fig. 6.26   Double-Post Zone Offense

The diagrams in figure 6.27 show various ways of using the tandem-post zone offense.

a. G1 passes to either P4 or F3. If the pass goes to P4, P4 looks for P5 or F3 for an opening. Overload opportunities are looked for. If P5 can shoot well facing the basket, she should move out on the baseline and face the basket.

b. If no shot is open, F3 passes to G1.

c. G1 passes to F2, while P4 and P5 cut across the lane in high and low post positions, respectively. F2 looks for a weak-side shot or for either P4 or P5 cutting.

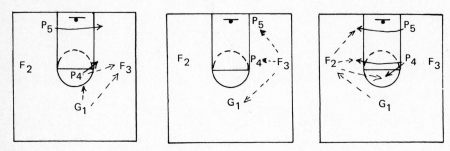

Fig. 6.27   Tandem-Post Zone Offense

The zone offense patterns shown above all work from an offensive 1-3-1 position. This alignment can be successful against almost all zones. Against the 2-3 zone the openings will usually be at the high post cut or at the forward weak-side shot. Against the 2-1-2 zone the openings will usually be in the low post position or the baseline overload or the forward outside shot. Against the 1-2-2 zone the attack can be made with the high post cutter or the weak-side screen and roll. These patterns are simple to execute, but are successful at all skill levels.

Patterns of defensive play

7

PLAYER-TO-PLAYER SYSTEM

The fundamentals of playing defense will be recalled from chapter 3. All these individual techniques fit into place in the team player-to-player defense.

In this defense each player is assigned to one opponent and uses her best defensive position and method on this player anywhere in the scoring area. Though a strict player-to-player defense is possible, a smart offense will take an advantage by use of cut-ins, screens, the give and go, and the pick-off and roll patterns. All of these offensive patterns are designed to maneuver the defensive player into a position in which she cannot adequately cover her assigned opponent. In these instances one of the defensive player's team-mates is usually available to cover the open player, so that a "switch" is called. When a defense makes those kinds of adjustments it has adapted to a *switch-ing player-to-player defense*.

Switching

The switching defense requires excellent teamwork and timing. Teammates must call out screens, pick-offs, and switches quickly to one another. If the defensive players have been assigned to offensive players to match certain abilities, these *match-ups* will be destroyed by random switching when it is not really necessary. In this case the *scissors crossover tactic* should be used when two opponents exchange positions or a cut is made that will be hard to follow. The crossover is made to allow space for the trapped defensive player to move to follow her assignment. The space is created by the defen-sive teammate who would otherwise have switched to pick up the open player. In this tactic it is never desirable for either player to be more than one body from their respective assignments. See figure 7.1.

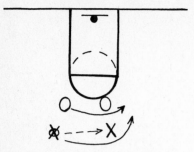
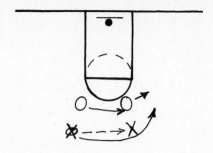

Fig. 7.1   The Scissors Crossover   Fig. 7.2   The Switch

When the scissors crossover is impossible or when match-ups are not a problem factor, a *switch* (fig. 7.2) is called when one defensive player cannot stay with her assignment. The "switch" is called by the teammate who will pick up the open player, since she can see the play develop and that her teammate is trapped. The defensive player who is obstructed from moving may see the need to switch too late to be able to adequately communicate to her teammate in time for the switch to be effective.

Defending the Pick-off and Roll

The *defense against the pick-off and roll* presents a special problem. As soon as the pick-off is set, the player on whom the screen has been set should make an adjustment. Either she should step in front of the pick-off to stay with her own assignment or she should step behind the pick-off to be able to switch and cover the roll.

Usually the defensive player who has been screened by the pick-off should step behind the pick-off screen. With this maneuver both the drive and the roll will be neutralized. If the ball handler can use the outside jump shot over the pick-off screen effectively, the player picked off must attempt to step over the front of the screen. This can be effective if the action is made aggressively and quickly.

Defending the Pivot Player

A *pivot player*, who assumes a position with her back to the basket and who is to be the hub of give-and-go patterns, is a difficult player to defend against. It is usually best for the pivot player's defender to play to the side of the pivot player with one hand up, discouraging the pass to the pivot player (fig. 7.3). Once a pass to the pivot player has been completed, the defender should drop back a step to see the whole play develop and if need be to switch to cover an open cutter.

The pivot player who is versatile in movement to the basket may be better defending by "fronting" (fig. 7.4). In this tactic the defensive player plays between the post player and the ball, attempting to discourage or intercept passes to her. This can be effective, since the passes to the "fronted" post

Fig. 7.3   Defending the Pivot Player—
Basic Positioning

Fig. 7.4   Defending the Pivot Player—
Fronting

player must capitalize on a high degree of accuracy for success. If the team-mates of the post player are weak in passing, the tactic may be highly successful.

Covering the Drive

Covering the drive is a special circumstance that must be predetermined by the team as a whole, for it has implications for the total team coordination. Either the defense will "take away the baseline" or will "invite to the baseline." In the former circumstance, the attempt is made to turn the driving player into the middle of the court where defensive teammates are available to help cover the play. In the latter, the attempt is to use the baseline to trap the player and limit the choices of the ball handler to either shoot from behind the plane of the backboard or to pass to only one side—the court side. If teammates of the ball defender are alert, the potential passing lane may be obstructed and an interception may be attempted.

Defending Against the Split Cut

Defensive coverage of the double split begins with the defender of the pivot player calling "pivot" or "high post" to warn her teammates who must cover the cutters (fig. 7.5). The players defending against the cutter should drop

What is the most important concept to keep in mind when employing a player-to-player defense?

Fig. 7.5   Defending the Split Cut

back a step toward the basket after the pass is completed to the pivot play. In this way they can automatically switch to cover the opposite cutter. If the cutters are not strong outside shooters an alternate defense can be established by having the cutters' defensive players sag and cover the pivot player from in front, thus completely stopping a pass to the pivot player.

Team Deployment and Coverage

To play a strong player-to-player defense, teamwork must be utilized to the maximum. Teammates must trust one another to cover specific situations in predetermined fashion, yet must be alert to step in and cover for a teammate pulled out of position or faked out by the offense. In every instance the concept that must be remembered is that the "ball must be covered." Often a player will see the ball handler open, but in effort to remain in a player-to-player coverage will hesitate to cover the ball. An offensive player should never be allowed to go to the basket without a defender challenging the play, whether or not the defender is the one originally assigned to the offensive player.

Team deployment in the player-to-player defense is built on the following principles: (1) the player defending against the ball handler should use strong defensive tactics; (2) the defenders adjacent to the ball handler should position to take away passing lanes to their respective offensive opponents; and (3) the defenders the greatest distance from the ball should shift toward the direction of the ball to assist their teammate in covering offensive cutters or closing up cutting lanes. This can be seen in figure 7.6.

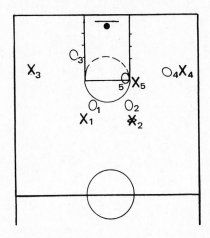

Fig. 7.6   Player-to-Player Defense—Coverage in Relation to the Ball

ZONE SYSTEMS

The second basic defense is the zone defense. The purpose of this defense is to cover the high-percentage scoring area completely by strategically placing one defensive player in each zone area. Each player will cover anyone in her zone who has the ball, while teammates adjust as the ball is moved about the court to try to stop passes into the high-percentage shooting areas. As the ball is moved around the court each player attempts to position in the portion of her zone nearest the ball.

The basic individual defensive tactics discussed in chapter 3 are used by all players in the zone defense as well. Each player defending against the player with the ball should move with that player's movements by sliding. Defensive players in zones away from the ball should attempt to cover the passing lanes to other offensive players. It is especially important that the zone immediately behind the one in which the ball is located be covered so that no offensive player is allowed a noncontested cut to the basket.

The zones in most common use for consideration here are the 2-3, the 2-1-2, and the 1-2-2 zones. There are several other zone deployments possible, but they have specialized uses and will not be discussed.

Which zone would you select in order to defend against a baseline attack? Against attack from the high post position? Against outside shooting?

The 2-3 and 2-1-2 zones are similar to one another, as seen in figures 7.7 and 7.8. Each covers a portion of the free throw lane with one player, and each has a two-player front. The major difference is that the 2-3 zone has more extended coverage at the baselines than does the 2-1-2.

The 1-2-2 (fig. 7.9) zone has extended coverage for outside shots, but is vulnerable in the middle of the free throw lane.

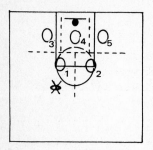 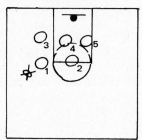 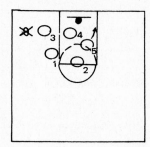

Fig. 7.7   The 2-3 Zone Defense

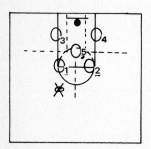 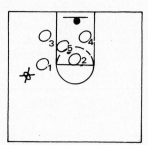 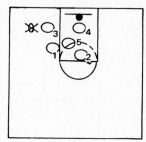

Fig. 7.8   The 2-1-2 Zone Defense

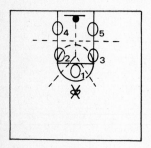 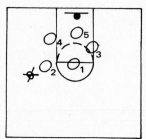 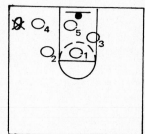

Fig. 7.9   The 1-2-2 Zone Defense

ZONE COVERAGE

In each diagram sequence shown, the dotted lines in the first diagram indicate the areas of the zone coverage. In each instance the dotted line should be considered somewhat flexible. As the ball is moved by the offensive each player should attempt to move to the part of her zone nearest the ball without pulling out of position. In addition, all players should work to intercept passes into or over the zone. The zone players can take more chances on interceptions than can the players in the player-to-player coverage, since there will always be teammates to back up the movement and the basket will thus always be covered.

ZONE STRENGTH

Each zone is selected for use depending on the needs to neutralize the opponents' strengths. The 2-3 zone is extremely effective against the low post and baseline attack to the basket. The 2-1-2 zone is less effective against the baseline attack, but is more effective in the low post and high post regions than the 2-3 zone. The 1-2-2 zone is extremely effective against all outside shooting. It is, however, vulnerable to attack from the high post position.

ZONE SELECTION

The appropriate zone should be selected in relation to the shooting capabilities of the opponents. For example, the opposing team has a tall player who moves near the basket; either the 2-3 or 2-1-2 zone would be effective. If the opponents had no one tall enough to infiltrate the zone the 1-2-2 might be effective.

Game situations

8

Under all circumstances each player must be alert to move from offense to defense quickly. Except in special situations the entire team should retreat to their own backcourt as soon as the opponents get possession of the ball. Their movement should be toward the backcourt free throw line, turning to meet the approaching opposition in good defensive position. This type of movement will help the team have a strong defense and make it very difficult for the opponents to start a fast break. The larger area of court used to defend the opponents, the easier will be their efforts to evade the defense. The pressing defense is reserved for special conditions, for highly conditioned teams, or for when your team is behind in score late in the game and possession of the ball is needed to score and catch up.

FAST BREAK

An advanced offensive technique is the *fast break*. This pattern is established when the defense gains possession of the ball. They pass the ball quickly up court, beating their opponents into the scoring area and usually have a breakaway, a 2-on-1, 3-on-2 or 4-on-3 ratio of offense to defense, and therefore an advantage to score.

The fast break requires excellent ball handling and the ability to execute skills while moving at high speed. It is unwise for inexperienced players to attempt this, since they will usually miscue and give the ball to the opponents on the error. In addition, the fast break requires great stamina. Because of the rapid movement it usually takes, after just five or six fast-break trips up and down the court, the average woman player is fatigued to the point of requiring a time-out for rest.

Do you know why the fast break is classified as an advanced technique?
How does the fast break begin?

The fast break begins with a defensive rebound, a jump ball tip, or an intercepted pass. The key to success in the fast break is a *quick clearout pass* and wise use of *court position* to gain advantage, along with *excellent ball handling* while on the move.

The *breakaway* is accomplished when one player can outrun and out-dribble the entire opposing team and score before the defense can recover. The breaking player should use her body to screen defenders behind her away from the ball as they seek to overtake her. She should also control and slow down her momentum as she goes to the basket for the lay-up shot so that the ball will not be shot too hard. In addition, she should attempt to approach the basket from her strongest shooting side.

The *two-on-one* fast break is shown in figure 8.1. The offensive players space just far enough apart as they progress into the front court so that the defender is unable to cover them both. As the defensive player commits her coverage to the ball handler, a pass is made to the open player for a score.

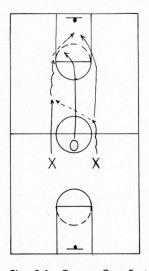

Fig. 8.1 Two-on-One Fast Break

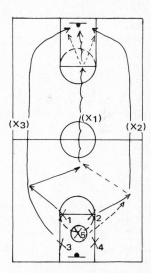

Fig. 8.2 Three-on-One Fast Break

The *three-on-one* or *three-on-two* fast break begins by centering the ball on court. Figure 8.2 shows this with a pass to a cutter to the center of the floor after a defensive rebound and a clear-out pass. The dribbler drives to the center of the court while two teammates fill a lane on either side of the court. As the free throw line is approached, the dribbler watches the defenders. If the defense comes to the ball, the dribbler will pass to the open player on either side. If the defender sags to watch the cutters on either side, the dribbler should continue to execute the basket herself.

FREE THROW SITUATIONS

In the *free throw situation* (fig. 8.3) both offense and defense should be alert to position themselves to their best advantage. The shooting team usually places one guard between the free throw line and the center line, ready to

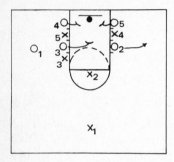

Fig. 8.3   Free Throw Line-ups

go back on defense should the opponents get the rebound. They should also place their tallest players in second spots on either side of the lane to attempt rebounds.

The defensive team positions its best two rebounders in the lane adjacent to the basket. These players work to screen out the opponents nearest them on the lane and recover the rebound. A third defender is placed so that she is able to move in front of the shooter on the rebound. The fourth defender may position herself on the lane line. The fifth player may be placed toward the sideline for a quick pass out to start a fast break.

JUMP BALL SITUATIONS

Jump ball situation positioning depends a great deal on whether your team expects to win the toss, lose it, or whether the result of the jump is mostly a matter of chance.

On the center jump ball to start each quarter the tallest player or best jumper (usually the center) should be the jumper. The diagram in figure 8.4 shows the suggested alignment. The slower of the two forwards, X4, plays toward her own offensive side of the circle. The faster of the forwards, X3, plays on the defensive side of the circle. The guards, X1 and X2, play on the sides of the circle, toward the offensive sides of the circle if they expect to win the toss and toward the defensive sides if they are in doubt about the outcome of the toss.

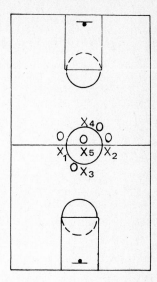

Fig. 8.4   Center Jump Ball Situation

The jump ball taken in the restraining circles requires the same considerations. If the team jumping in their own backcourt expects to win the toss, the members may position as in figure 8.5. If they expect to lose the toss, or if the outcome is fairly uncertain, they should position for defense, as in figure 8.6.

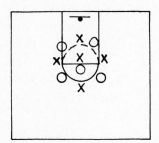

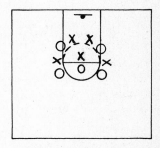

Fig. 8.5   Backcourt Jump Ball
—Offensive Advantage

Fig. 8.6   Backcourt Jump Ball
—Defensive Advantage

BIBLIOGRAPHY

Cousy, Bob, and Power, Frank, Jr. *Basketball Concepts and Techniques.* Boston: Allyn and Bacon, 1970.

Wilkes, Glenn. *Basketball for Men.* 3d ed. Dubuque, Ia.: Wm. C. Brown Company Publishers, 1977.

Wooden, John. *Practical Modern Basketball.* New York: The Ronald Press, 1966.

Rules of the game

9

The rules of basketball have changed through the years. As the game has developed and new styles of play inaugurated, it has been necessary to adjust the rules accordingly. It is essential for a player to make a careful study of the rules each year to keep in touch with changes as they occur.

BASIC REQUIREMENTS

The Court
The *basketball court* (fig. 9.1) has several specific markings that should be identified. The court is divided in half by a *center line*. Three large *restraining circles*, each with a radius of 6 feet, are placed strategically on the court. One is placed at the center of the court. The other two are located with their cen-

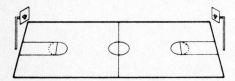

Fig. 9.1   The Basketball Court

ters 15 feet from the basket. The restraining circles at either end of the court are divided in half by lines that run parallel to the end lines of the court. These are the *free throw lines*. Lines, starting at the free throw line and running tangent to the circles extend to the end lines. These lines and the free throw line make up the *free throw lane*.

The Team
Each *team* is composed of five players who may play the entire court area.

The Game

The *game* is composed of two twenty-minute *halves*. There is a fifteen-minute intermission between halves. The *playing time* is continuous except that the clock is stopped when violations, fouls, or jump balls occur and when time-out for rest or substitution is called. The offensive team is timed for *thirty seconds* when in possession of the ball. When this rule is used it is a violation to fail to attempt a shot within thirty seconds after taking possession of the ball.

Scoring

A team *scores* two points when the ball passes through the basket in regular play. This is known as a *field goal.* A *free throw* is awarded a team as a result of certain infractions of rules by their opponents. If made, this basket scores one point. The *winner* of the game is the team who leads at the end of the second half. If the game is *tied*, the winner is determined by playing one or more extra play periods, each of which is three minutes in length and preceded by two minutes of rest.

PLAYING THE GAME

Each *half is started* with a jump ball in the center circle. On the *jump ball* an official tosses the ball upward between two opponents, each of whom must be on her own half of the circle and facing her own goal. All teammates of the jumpers must be outside the restraining circles until the ball is tapped. The ball may be tapped twice by the jumpers, but neither may catch it until it has touched another player or the floor.

Once a team has gained possession of the ball *any player* may throw, pass, bounce, or roll the ball to another teammate; she may shoot for a basket or she may bounce the ball successively to herself while moving. She may hold the ball up to five seconds while she is closely guarded, then she must pass it. In addition, she may pivot with the ball and she may take two steps to stop upon catching the ball on the run or in stopping after a dribble. It is also legal for a player to *tie the ball* by placing one or both hands firmly on it while it is in the possession of another player. It is also legal to take or tap the ball from an opponent. If a tie ball occurs, a jump ball is taken by the two players involved at the nearest restraining circle.

After a field goal is scored the opponents of the scoring team put the ball back into play by taking it out-of-bounds under the opponent's goal.

Rule Infractions—Violations

There are a number of things a *player may not do*. These are categorized into major and minor infractions of the rules. The minor infractions are called *violations*. If a violation occurs, the opponents are awarded possession of the ball out-of-bounds at the sideline or end line nearest to where the infraction was made. If one member of each team commits a violation at the same time, a jump ball is taken in the nearest restraining circle.

Can you think of several basketball rules in which the number five appears?

It is a violation to: (1) cause the ball to go out-of-bounds; (2) hold the ball for more than 5 seconds while being closely guarded, more than 5 seconds while out-of-bounds, or more than 10 seconds before shooting a free throw; (3) touch a boundary line while in possession of the ball; (4) kick the ball intentionally; (5) walk with the ball, other than in connection with the legal pivot or two-step stop; (6) touch the ball with more than one hand on other than the first bounce of a dribble; (7) tap the ball on a jump ball more than twice or before it reaches its highest point on the toss; (8) catch the ball on a jump ball; (9) fail to stay in one's own half of the circle on a jump ball until the ball is tapped; (10) enter the restraining circle before the ball is tapped on a jump ball; (11) change positions until a jump ball is tossed if the player is one positioned around the restraining circle; (12) have a player without the ball stay in the free throw lane for more than 3 seconds while her team has possession of the ball in it's own frontcourt; and (13) have possession of the ball in the free throw lane for more than 3 seconds without shooting or moving out of lane.

Rule Infractions—Fouls

Major infractions of the rules are called *fouls*. For the first six fouls for each team in each half, the opponents are awarded the ball out-of-bounds at the sideline or end line nearest the play. For the seventh foul for a team and each foul thereafter in each half the opponents shoot free throws. If the player is fouled, other than in the act of shooting, she is awarded one free throw and if this free throw is made, she is awarded an additional free throw. This situation is called the *one plus one*. If the player is fouled in the act of shooting she is awarded two free throws if the basket is missed and one free throw if the basket is made. *Exception*: No free throws are awarded when an offensive player commits a foul, though these fouls do count in the cumulative team fouls. Two free throws are also awarded when a player commits a *flagrant foul* (unsportsmanlike conduct of a violent nature) or an *intentional foul*. If the flagrant foul should occur, the player is disqualified from the game and the team offended also gets possession of the ball out-of-bounds at the midcourt line.

Fouls in which contact occurs that are not flagrant or intentional are called *common fouls*. Fouls in which no contact occurs by a player or nonplayer are called *technical fouls*. If a technical foul is called, the team offended may choose any player to shoot the free throw, and the shooting team receives the ball out-of-bounds at the midcourt line.

It is a common foul to: (1) block—interfere with the movement of an opponent with personal contact; (2) charge—a player with the ball moves into an opponent who has already established a position or path of movement; (3) trip; (4) push; (5) hold; and (6) hack.

It is a technical foul to: (1) disrespectfully address an official; (2) delay the game; (3) fail to raise the hand after being called for a foul; (4) substitute illegally; (5) take more than the legal number of time-outs; (6) incite undesirable crowd reactions; and (7) a number of other similar acts of unsportsmanlike and unethical behavior spelled out in the official rules.

If two opponents foul simultaneously, each offending player is assessed a common foul and the game is restarted with a center jump ball between any two players.

Free Throws

A *free throw* is an unguarded shot for goal from a point behind the free throw line; if made it scores one point. The free throw is taken by the player fouled. During the free throw the teams line up along the free throw lane in alternating positions. The first spot on the line nearest the goal may be occupied by the defensive team. The second spot on the line may be occupied by the offensive team. If the basket is scored, the opponents are given the ball out-of-bounds at the end line under the basket. If the basket is missed, the ball is considered in play as soon as it touches the rim of the basket and each team may attempt to gain its possession. The players lined up for the rebound may not enter the lane before the ball touches the rim or enters the basket.

It is a violation on the free throw to: (1) touch any part of the lane line or beyond it until the ball touches the rim of the basket; (2) hold the ball more than 10 seconds before shooting; (3) fail to cause the ball to touch the rim of the basket or enter the basket.

When a violation is committed by the offense, the opponents are given the ball out-of-bounds at the sideline opposite the free throw line, and the goal, if made, is not allowed. If the violation is committed by a defensive player, the shot, if missed, is repeated. If it is made, the defense is awarded the ball out-of-bounds as if no violation had occurred. When more than one free throw is awarded and a violation is committed by the defense on the first shot, the basket, if made, is allowed; if missed, it is repeated. In this same instance, if the offense commits the violation, the goal is not allowed. In any case, the ball is put back into play with reference to what occurs on the last free throw.

Disqualification

A player is *disqualified* from the game upon receiving five fouls. In addition, a single disqualifying foul may be called for unsportsmanlike conduct or unnecessary roughness.

Time-outs

Each team may call five *time-outs* during the course of a game. Each time-out is one minute in length. One additional time-out is permitted for each overtime period. Time-out may be called any time the ball is dead or when the team requesting time-out has possession of the ball.

What opportunities to play basketball are available in your community? Which levels of skill and which age groups are served?

Substitutions

Substitutions may be made at any time the ball is dead, and a time-out of 30 seconds is taken to complete the change. The player should report to the scorer and then wait to be called onto the court by the official, thus completing the substitution.

OFFICIAL RULES

Because basketball for girls and women in the United States has developed on a somewhat regional basis, numerous sets of rules have been used to regulate play in different parts of the country. The major differences in these rules do not radically affect the appearance of the game, but are, for the most part, related to details in the conduct of the game.

The most commonly used set of rules in schools and colleges is that provided by the National Association for Girls and Women's Sports of the American Alliance for Health, Physical Education, and Recreation. These rules are identical with those used to govern all play conducted under the auspices of the Amateur Athletic Union. Guides for basketball, which include the official rules, are published yearly by both of these organizations. Copies are available from the American Alliance for Health, Physical Education, and Recreation, 1201 Sixteenth Street, N.W., Washington, D. C. The Amateur Athletic Union distributes guides through each regional office of the association. A local directory should give specific information in regard to the location of the office nearest you.

OFFICIATING

The official is a vital part of each basketball game. There are two officials responsible for the conduct of a game—the referee and umpire—who make the calls in reference to play. They are assisted by two scorers and two timers. Each person in this group has specific duties that are outlined in detail in the official rules.

The National Association for Girls and Women's Sports has a subcommittee, the Officiating Services Division, which establishes standards and techniques for officials. The Officiating Services Division is a national body, which regulates officiating for girls' and women's sports. Local officiating organizations can become affiliated with this national group. These local organizations, or boards of officials, are active in training and certifying officials, as well as supplying officials to any school or agency requesting the services of trained officials. The affiliated boards of officials currently certify or give three classifications, or ratings, for officials. In rank order they are the National,

State, and Apprentice ratings. Each classification denotes the attainment of an established level of knowledge and ability.

Each *Basketball Guide* published by the American Alliance for Health, Physical Education, and Recreation contains complete information in regard to techniques and standards for officiating and the names and addresses of the officers of every affiliated board of officials in the United States.

If you are interested in becoming an official, you should study the official rules carefully and practice officiating according to the prescribed procedure. Contact your local board of officials for opportunities to practice with the help of trained officials. After the training period you can obtain one of the ratings listed by successfully completing a written test and a practical test.

The Amateur Athletic Union also certifies officials for their competitions. Through a working agreement between the two organizations, any Officiating Services Division official may register as an AAU official, maintaining the same rating.

A basic understanding of the rules is necessary for good play. Learn the essentials, and work to keep the pace of the game moving by responding appropriately when the official makes decisions.

REFERENCE

NAGWS Basketball Guide, 1976-77. Washington, D. C.: American Alliance for Health, Physical Education, and Recreation.

Appendix: Questions and answers

MULTIPLE CHOICE

1. If the wrist action of the chest pass has been correctly performed, the following should be evident in the follow-through.
   a. The elbows will be below shoulder height.
   b. The wrists will be fully flexed.
   C. The palms of the hands will face downward. (p. 16)

2. One of the advantages of the bounce pass is that it
   a. can be used to cover long distances
   B. lends deception to passing tactics
   c. can be used in congested court space (p. 18)

3. To protect the ball from a defensive opponent the offensive player should
   a. stay at least three feet away from opponents
   B. keep the ball close to the body with arms and elbows away from the body
   c. dribble whenever possible (pp. 20, 21)

4. A key to maintaining control of the ball while attempting to out-position an opponent with a dribble is that of
   a. pushing the ball so that it will rebound to above waist height
   b. maintaining a constant height for each bounce in the dribble
   C. bouncing the ball to rebound between knee and waist height (p. 21)

5. The one-hand set shot is desirable as a shooting technique because
   A. preparation time for the shot is very short
   b. it can be easily mastered
   c. it takes little strength to execute (p. 23)

6. Increased power for the one-hand set shot is developed for use at greater distances from the basket by
   A. bending the knees deeply and pushing the feet forcefully from the floor
   b. dropping the ball downward to wind up prior to the upward push for the shot
   c. transferring the weight forcefully from rear foot to forward foot (p. 24)

7. The force required to carry the ball to the basket on a lay-up shot is obtained
   A. from the momentum of the player's movement toward the basket transferred to the ball upon release
   b. the strong upward thrust of the arms used to elevate the ball toward the basket
   c. the sharp wrist action used to release the ball against the backboard   (p. 26)

8. An offensive player could attempt to drive to the basket to score against an opponent (player-to-player defense) who
   a. establishes a position between the offensive player and the basket
   b. uses a balanced forward stride stance
   C. positions with legs and trunk held erect   (p. 42)

9. Defensive positioning and movement against an opponent attempting an offensive drive is to
   a. step into the path of the player as soon as she begins to move
   b. move alongside the offensive player, following her path
   C. move in a straight line to the spot to which the offensive player will eventually come   (p. 30)

10. To counteract advance offensive play the defensive player should
    A. attempt to force the offensive player into the least desirable movement patterns
    b. position as close as possible to the offensive player at all times
    c. consistently position between her opponent and the ball   (p. 39)

11. Cardiorespiratory endurance for sustained movement and performance is developed by
    a. exercising to a fatigue state at each practice
    B. participating in an activity schedule that is progressively more physiologically demanding
    c. participating in a weight-training program   (p. 12)

12. After establishing a screen, the screener should
    a. hold the arms out at shoulder level
    b. position as close to the shooter as possible
    C. be alert to move to the basket if defenders slip around the screen   (p. 47)

13. The pick-off and roll tactic is vulnerable to developing an offensive foul if
    A. the drive starts before the screen is in a stationary position
    b. the roll option is delayed momentarily
    c. the defensive players switch assignments promptly   (p. 49)

14. The zone defense is usually ineffective against
    a. the give and go
    B. long shots
    c. the cut-in   (p. 56)

15. A player-to-player defensive tactic used to defend against the pivot player is
    a. the scissors when she has the ball
    b. to play directly behind her when she is without the ball
    C. to play to one side of her to attempt to block passes to her   (p. 62)

16. A player should be called for a traveling violation if she
    a. pivots, repeatedly moving one foot while keeping the other in a set position
    B. lifts her pivot foot and returns it to the court before releasing the ball
    c. takes two steps in stopping after completing a dribble   (pp. 6, 74)

17. A technical foul is called if a player
    A. delays the game in an unnecessary manner
    b. remains in the free throw lane longer than three seconds when her team has the ball in its frontcourt
    c. catches the ball while participating in a jump ball   (p. 75)

18. A field goal is not allowed if
    A. the shooter fouls an opponent before she is in the act of shooting

b. the shooter is fouled in the last two minutes of the game
c. the shooter is fouled just before she releases the ball for the shot   (p. 74)

19. During a free throw players line up along the free throw lane so that
A. the defensive team members occupy the first spot at each side of the lane
b. each team occupies one spot adjacent to the goal
c. the defensive team chooses the side of lane in which a player will occupy the spot adjacent to the goal   (p. 75)

20. It is a violation if during a free throw
a. the shooter holds the ball more than five seconds
b. any player touches the lane lines after the ball touches the rim of the basket
C. the shooter fails to cause the ball to touch the rim of the basket or enter the basket   (p. 75)

21. It is a common foul if a player
a. repeatedly contacts an opponent lightly with the hand or arm to locate her position
B. makes noise while an opponent is shooting a free throw
c. blocks an opponent with physical contact   (p. 74)

22. If a violation occurs during regular play the opponents of the offending team should receive
A. possession of the ball out of bounds at the sideline or endline nearest the spot where the violation occurred
b. a free throw
c. possession of the ball at the sideline opposite the free throw line   (p. 73)

23. An illegal dribble is called if a player
a. fumbles a pass, picks up the ball, and then dribbles
B. touches the ball with two hands on the second bounce
c. bounces the ball first with the right hand and then with the left hand   (p. 74)

24. If a game ends in a tie the winner is determined by
a. continuing play until one team scores a field goal
b. playing one extra play period which is two minutes in length
C. playing one or more extra play periods which are three minutes in length   (p. 73)

25. A violation is called if
a. a player participating in a jump ball catches the ball after it has touched the floor
B. the ball is held for more than five seconds on an out-of-bounds play
c. a player attempts to shoot for a goal from the backcourt   (p. 74)

TRUE OR FALSE

T f 26. One of the disadvantages of the chest pass is that most girls and women can use it effectively at limited distances.   (p. 16)

t F 27. The one-hand underhand pass should be used primarily for long-distance passes.   (p. 16)

t F 28. Passes should be aimed to the area between a teammate's knees and waist for most effective handling.   (p. 20)

t F 29. The ball may be touched with either hand or both hands on successive bounces of the dribble.   (p. 21)

T f 30. A two-footed take-off is recommended in jumping for rebounding to insure control of the body in limited space.   (p. 12)

t F 31. For the one-hand set shot the feet are placed in a forward stride stance with the foot opposite the shooting hand in the forward position.   (p. 23)

T f 32. On the lay-up shot the ball is released by the shooting hand at full extension of the body in the leap and reach toward the basket.   (p. 26)

T f   33. An object (the ball) will rebound from a surface at an angle equal to that at which it approaches that surface.   (p. 27)

T f   34. Fake movements prior to shooting, passing, or moving are most effective if done in varying sequence and direction.   (p. 28)

T f   35. A player who scores three shots in five attempted field goals is considered to be very successful.   (p. 30)

t F   36. After securing an offensive rebound the player should bring the ball down and close to the body.   (p. 31)

T f   37. When playing a normal player-to-player defense a defender should establish a stance between the opponent and the basket.   (p. 29)

t F   38. A strong defensive player should jump in an attempt to block each movement made upward by her offensive opponent.   (p. 30)

T f   39. One key to strong defensive play is the use of verbal communication among team members.   (p. 62)

t F   40. After an offensive opponent has attempted a shot, defensive players should move to a position directly under the basket to obtain the rebound.   (p. 32)

T f   41. After gaining possession of the ball on a defensive rebound a quick pass to a teammate is preferred to dribbling the ball.   (p. 32)

t F   42. The defensive player in a player-to-player defense who is defending a player away from the ball should position so that her body is between her opponent and the ball.   (p. 30)

T f   43. The fall-away shot is limited in advantage because the shooter is off-balance and is usually unable to assist in rebounding.   (p. 36)

T f   44. In order to shoot effectively in late stages of the game, it is recommended that players practice shooting after an exhaustive portion of a practice session. (p. 13)

t F   45. A player should practice to score free throws more frequently than shots from various angles and distances.   (p. 13)

T f   46. For the cut-in pattern to be effective the cutting player must create space for her cutting movement by faking or drawing her opponent out of position.   (p. 28)

t F   47. Screening is used in order to give the offensive team a better opportunity to gain rebounds.   (p. 46)

t F   48. The defense designed to match the individual speed and height of players to that of opponents is called a zone defense.   (p. 61)

t F   49. When a player in a player-to-player defense cannot follow her assigned opponent she should begin to defend the opponent nearest to her.   (p. 61)

T f   50. In playing a zone defense all defenders should move and adjust on the court in relation to the position of the ball.   (p. 65)

T f   51. The zone defense is vulnerable to penetration if players in rear zones fail to back up the position of teammates who have moved to defend against the ball handler.   (p. 65)

t F   52. The zone defense eliminates most opportunities for an offense to score with long shots.   (p. 56)

T f   53. The player-to-player defense is vulnerable to cutting and driving patterns. (p. 61)

T f   54. A pivot offense is designed to take advantage of the attributes of one tall player on a team.   (p. 51)

t F   55. The fast break, an effective technique to gain a quick score, is simple for the beginner to master.   (p. 68)

T f   56. On the breakaway the ball handler should try to stay in the middle of the floor.   (p. 69) t F   57. During a free throw all the nonshooting teammates of the shooter should line up for the rebound. (p. 70)

T f   58. During a jump ball each jumper may tap the ball only twice. (p. 74)

T f   59. A player may take the ball away from an opponent provided no personal contact occurs. (p. 73)

t F   60. If a player in the act of shooting is fouled by her opponent and makes the field goal, she is awarded two free throws. (p. 74)

COMPLETION

61. To increase the effectiveness of passing, the use of (*faking*) movements must become a part of basic ball-handling skills. (p. 27)

62. A player with the ball who desires to move about on the court while maintaining possession of the ball does so by using a (*dribble*). (p. 5)

63. For good body control in movement the body weight should be kept (*low*). (p. 10)

64. To legally move in place while in possession of the ball the footwork technique called a (*pivot*) is used. (p. 6)

65. The ball can easily be banked from the backboard into the basket on set shots taken at angles between (*20-45*) degrees to the backboard. (p. 25)

66. The term (*cutting*) refers to the movement of an offensive player without the ball into an open space on the court. (p. 28)

67. The movement of a player with the ball to dribble toward the basket is called a (*drive*). (p. 5)

68. The shooting technique most commonly mastered by advanced players is the (*jump*) shot. (p. 33)

69. In the (*hook or turnaround*) shot the advanced player starts with her back to the basket. (p. 36)

70. The skill used to tap a rebounded ball into a quick return shot is called a (*tip-in*). (p. 38)

71. The advanced pass which can be effectively used in close quarters is the (*hook or jump*) pass. (pp. 35, 36)

72. One of the major advantages of the hook shot is that it is (*impossible to defend*). (p. 35)

73. In the jump shot the basket is sighted (*under*) the ball. (p. 33)

74. The ability of the body systems to adapt and function when sustained demands are imposed is called (*endurance*). (p. 12)

75. The two-player offensive pattern called the (*give and go*) is one in which Player A passes to Player B who then executes a return pass to A who has moved into an advantageous position. (p. 46)

76. In offensive tactics the positioning of one offensive player between a teammate with the ball and her defender to give a free moment to shoot is called (*screening*). (pp. 6, 47)

77. The (*player-to-player*) defense is one in which each defensive player is assigned to guard against a specific opponent. (p. 61)

78. The (*zone*) defense is designed to cover the scoring area of the court by placing individual defenders in specific spaces of the court. (p. 65)

79. The zone defense which covers the middle of the key in addition to covering outside shots to a degree is the (*2-1-2 or 2-3*) defense. (p. 67)

80. The zone defense stifles an offense built around (*cutting*) offensive patterns. (p. 67)

81. The basic offensive organization from which team tactics are begun is called (*floor position*).   (p. 51)
82. Taller players who shoot well facing the basket should be positioned as (*forwards*) in the single post offense.   (p. 51)
83. An offensive player who positions with her back to the basket in close proximity to the basket is said to be playing a (*low post*) position.   (p. 52)
84. When an offensive player positions with her back to the basket at free throw distance from the basket to be a hub for passes and cutting she is considered to be playing the (*high post*) position.   (p. 52)
85. The pivot offense with cutting options is most effective against a (*player-to-player*) defense.   (p. 53)
86. In order to draw a zone defense away from the basket so that openings occur for short-range shots it is necessary to score (*long*) shots.   (p. 56)
87. A team tactic used to move the ball to the offensive end of the court before the opponents can set up a defense is called (*fast break*).   (p. 68)
88. The originator of the game of basketball was (*Naismith*).   (p. 1)
89. The major rule-making bodies for women's basketball rules are (*NAGWS and AAU*).   (p. 76)
90. If a player passes to a teammate for an immediate score she should be credited with a(n) (*assist*).   (p. 4)
91. When two teammates simultaneously guard one opponent with the ball they are executing a (*double-team*) tactic.   (p. 5)
92. A (*turnover*) occurs when the team with the ball loses possession without having taken a shot at the basket.   (p. 6)
93. The center point of the free throw line is (*15*) feet from the basket.   (p. 72)
94. Minor infractions of the rules for which the opponents are awarded the ball out-of-bounds are called (*violations*).   (p. 73)
95. After a tie ball the ball is put into play with a (*jump ball*).   (p. 73)
96. A player who receives a pass while moving is allowed (*two*) steps to come to a stop.   (p. 73)
97. A defensive player who interferes with the movement of an opponent causing personal contact has committed a (*blocking*) foul.   (p. 74)
98. An offensive foul caused when a player with the ball moves into and contacts a defensive player who has an established position is called (*charging*).   (p. 74)
99. A player is disqualified from the game when she has accumulated (*five*) fouls. (p. 75)
100. The major international competition in which women's basketball is played is the (*Pan-American Games or Olympic Games*).   (p. 2)

ANSWERS TO EVALUATION QUESTIONS

*No answer

Page	Answer and Page Reference
3	1976 in Montreal, Canada; Pan-American Games, World Games, World University Games. (p. 2)
4	Free-lance: players attempting to take advantage of offensive situations as they occur; gunner: a shooter who shoots almost every time she has the ball; hot-hand: a shooter who is scoring with regularity; give and go: a play pattern in which a player passes and cuts to receive a return pass; cripple: an unguarded high percentage shot; solo: a one-player effort on offense. (pp. 5-6)

5   Rules suggestions should be sent to the National Association for Girls and Women's Sports or Amateur Athletic Unions Basketball Committees.   (p. 3)

11   The pivot.   (pp. 6, 11-12)

17   *

19   Advantages: Tall players can direct pass to teammate over shorter defensive players. Disadvantages: In congested areas the ball can be easily tied or stolen.
Protect the ball by keeping it directly overhead with elbows out to the sides and use a broad forward stride stance.   (p. 19)

21   *

23   The front of the rim of the basket.   (p. 25)

27   Errors occurs if
a. in a head, shoulder, or foot fake the body weight is shifted toward the fake
b. the ball follows the faking movement of a body part
c. fakes are unconvincing
d. the same sequence and direction of movements are used repeatedly (pp. 27-28)

28   *

32   Aiming is more difficult since the player starts with her back to the basket and must pivot and turn her head before the basket is sighted.   (pp. 35-36)

38   The most important factor on the tip-in is timing the jump.   (p. 38)

43   Defensive errors that can be exploited by the player with the ball are
a. standing too erectly
b. overshifting weight to one foot
c. jumping to block the ball
d. overanxiously reacting to fakes
e. crossing feet when changing direction
f. putting weight on heels when stopping or changing direction
g. bringing body too close to offensive player outside 18 foot radius to basket   (p. 42)

45   *

56   *

64   Teamwork: coordination, communication, and switching to insure the coverage of the ball.   (p. 64)

66   The baseline attack is best defended with a 2-3 zone; the high post attack is best defended with the 2-1-2 zone; good outside shooting is best defended with the 1-2-2 zone.   (p. 67)

69   The fast break requires excellent ball handling and the ability to execute skills at high speed.   (p. 68)

74   a. Five players on a team
b. Player cannot hold the ball more than 5 seconds while closely guarded or out-of-bounds.
c. Player is disqualified when she receives 5 fouls.   (pp. 72-75)

76   *

Index

Aiming
   passing, 18, 20
   shooting, 25
Amateur Athletic Union, 2, 76, 77
Assist, 4
Attitude, 13-14

Back door cut, 45-46
Backcourt, 5
Backspin, 19, 24
Ball control, 5
Ball handling 15-23
Body control, 10
   changing direction, 11
   jumping, 12
   pivoting, 11
   running, 11
   sliding, 11
   starting, 10-11
   stopping, 11
Bounce pass, 18-19

Changing direction, 11
Chest pass, 15-16
Conditioning, 12
Continuity, 53
Control dribble, 21
Court size, 72
Cripple, 5
Crossover dribble, 37
Current trends, 2-3

Cuts, 5, 44-46
   back door, 45-46
   front door, 45-46
   split, 46
Cutting, 28

Defense 5, 28-30
   against the drive, 63
   against pick-off and roll, 62
   against player with ball, 29
   against player without ball, 30
   against the post player, 62
   against the split cut, 63-64
   basic concepts, 40-41
   forcing opponent's choices, 39
   positioning, 28
   rebounding, 30-31
Defensive patterns
   player-to-player, 61-65
   zone, 65-67
Double post, 52, 59-60
Double split, 49
Double-team, 5
Dribble, 5, 21-22, 37-38
   control, 21
   crossover, 37
   reverse pivot, 37
   speed, 22
Drive, 5, 42-43

Endurance, 12

Faking, 5, 27
Fall-away shot, 5, 36
Fast break, 5, 68-69
  breakaway, 69
  three-on-two, 69
  two-on-one, 69
Feint, 5
Flexibility, 12
Floor position, 51-52
  double post, 52
  single post, 51
  tandem post, 52
Forward, 51-52
Fouls, 74-75
Free throws, 70, 75
  game situations, 70
  violations, 75
Free-lance, 5, 53
Frontcourt, 5

Game, 73
Game situations, 68-71
Give and go, 5, 46
Guard, 51
Gunner, 5

High post, 52
History, 1-2
Hook pass, 36
Hook shot, 5, 35
Hot hand, 5

International play, 2-3

Jam and release, 43
Jump ball situations, 5, 70
Jump pass, 35
Jump shot, 33
Jumping, 12

Lay-up shot, 6, 25-26
Learning, 9
Low post, 52

Moves, 6

National Association for Girls and Women's Sports, 2, 76, 77

Offense
  attacking player-to-player defense, 53-55
  attacking zone defense, 56-60

  basic concepts, 40-41
  rebounding, 31-32
  three-player patterns, 49-50
  two-player patterns, 44-49
Official rules, 72, 76
One-hand overhead pass, 17-18
One-hand set shot, 23
One-hand underhand pass, 16
One-on-one, 6, 42-44
  with the ball, 42-43
  without the ball, 43-44
Organizing the offense, 51
Overloading the zone, 57

Passing, 15-20
  bounce pass, 18-19
  chest pass, 15-16
  jump pass, 35
  one-hand overhand, 17-18
  one-hand underhand, 16
  receiving passes, 20-21
  two-hand overhead, 19
Pattern play, 6, 53-60
Percentage play, 6, 40-41
Pick-off, 6, 50
Pivot, 6, 11-12
Player-to-player defense, 61-65
  scissors crossover, 61-62
  switch, 61-62
Post, 6, 52
Practice, 13
Press, 6
Protecting the ball, 20-21

Ready position, 10-11
Rebounding
  defensive, 30-31
  offensive, 31-32
Reverse dribble, 37
Running, 11

Scissors crossover, 61-62
Screen, 6, 46-47
Semicontinuity, 53
Set shots, 6
  one-hand, 23
  two-hand, 25
Shooting, 23-27
  fall-away, 36
  hook shot, 36
  jump shot, 33
  lay-up, 25-26
  one-hand set shot, 23
  practice, 13

tip-in, 38
two-hand overhead, 27
two-hand set shot, 25
Single-post offense, 51-53, 54-55, 57-59
Sliding, 11
Solo, 5
Sportsmanship, 14
Strength, 12
Substitution, 76
Switch, 61-62

Tandem post, 52, 59-61
Three-player patterns, 49-50
Time out, 75
Tip-in, 38
Topspin, 19
Turnaround shot, 36
Turnover, 6
Two-hand overhead pass, 19

Two-hand overhead shot, 27
Two-player patterns, 44-49
    back door cut, 45-46
    front door cut, 44-45
    give and go, 5, 46
    screen and roll, 6, 46-47
    screens, 6, 47

Violations, 73-74

Warm-up, 13
Weakside, 66

Zone defense, 6, 65-67
    selection, 67
    strength, 67
    vulnerability, 56
Zone offense, 56-60